BAL

KT-222-954

Self.Styled

Self.Styled

DARE TO BE DIFFERENT

Anthony Lycett

jacqui small

First published in 2016 by

Jacqui Small LLP
74–77 White Lion Street
London N1 9PF

Publisher: Jacqui Small

Senior Commissioning Editor

Managing Editor: Emma Hey

Designer: Tim Barnes

Editor: Justyn Barnes

Production: Maeve Healy

ISBN: 9781910254752

A catalogue record for this book is available
from the British Library.

2018 2017 2016

10 9 8 7 6 5 4 3 2 1

Printed in China

Quarto is the authority on a wide range of topics.
Quarto educates, entertains and enriches the lives of
our readers – enthusiasts and lovers of hands-on living.
www.QuartoKnows.com

Contents

Foreword

What does it mean to put one's self on show? Anthony Lycett's glorious presentation of sartorial exhibitionism in the second decade of the 21st century provides some very affirmative responses.

Art and fashion historians would argue that the presentation of self through clothing and adornment is nothing new. Painters and photographers have been trading on swagger for generations. But there is something particular in these portraits that capture an extended moment, one that stretches back perhaps as far as the Devonshire House Diamond Jubilee Fancy Dress Ball of 1897, via the Chelsea Arts Balls that ran, often scandalously, in the Albert Hall from 1908 to 1958, via Strange and Egan's Blitz club and Leigh Bowery's Taboo of the early to mid 1980s.

There are ghosts and echoes of all of that London aptitude for dressing *up* in Anthony's diptychs, though in 2016 the scope is broader, the global connections more expansive and the cultural referencing more diverse than was ever possible in the pre-worldwide-web days of the 20th century.

The do-it-yourself impulse is clearly still there, alongside the devoted passion for self-transformation. Yet there is also something more vivid, persistent and defiantly celebratory in these *Self.Styled* portraits. I am left rather humbled by their candidly extrovert quality. Sociologists tell me that 'identity' – meaning embodied identity relating to race, age, sexuality and, particularly, gender – has become the last remaining terrain for serious culture war.

If transgression and freedom from an imposition of the so-called 'norm' is the desired endgame in this war, then some of the subjects pictured here make for fine strategists, generals and shock troops.

Their assertive 'take me as you see me and tremble' stance is full of visual and corporeal power.

Beyond the big historical and social themes there is also a micro-story in this collection. The individual choices of cut, style, detail, accessory, textile, jewel, cosmetic, feather and curl on show here are staggering in their precision and diversity. It is a rich book of costume, whose plates remind me of those Renaissance woodcuts of costumes across the known world, with a few demons and angels thrown in for good measure. Historians 500 years hence may well come across these technicoloured fantasies and wonder.

For setting such a moment and a community down on paper for posterity, Anthony, his sitters and his publishers are to be congratulated. I can see the love in it and I can also see that putting yourself on show is an act that goes to the heart of what it means to be human. When I was young enough and close enough to go to London clubs I was part afraid, part in awe and part in envy of those who took dressing to impress to its extremes. *Self.Styled* brings some of those mixed-up feelings back, but also leaves me smiling and grateful that the art of dressing up is still flourishing.

Christopher Breward
Principal, Edinburgh College of Art
Vice Principal, Creative Industries and
Performing Arts, University of Edinburgh

Anthony Lycett & Karina Akopyan

"I am me and not them"

In 2008, I was doing a lot of fashion shoots for *Flux* magazine. The stylist and I were always looking for interesting characters, rather than commercial-looking models. I thought they looked great when they turned up, but then we dressed them up to suit the whims of the labels that advertised in the magazine. The world these characters came from seemed more interesting than the world I was creating with them in fashion.

They weren't famous people, but they had a certain way of presenting themselves. They weren't following trends and I wanted to learn more about them. That was where the *Self.Styled* project evolved from and eight years on it still continues.

I began with the idea of celebrating people with the courage to express themselves in this way. It turned into almost an examination, because I became so interested in the particular details of each individual. To focus in on these, I decided to shoot everyone on a plain white background. This set-up means they can come to my studio, or I can take the set-up to them. By taking people out of the context of their normal daily life, you focus more on their character, the way they dress.

That is the extent to which I control the image, by the fact that I create the same universe – the same background, the same lighting – for everyone, but I relinquish control of direction. I never art-direct them to stand a certain way. Whether they appear quite unsure or there is an explosion of expression, it comes from them.

The only clothing brief I give each person in advance is to bring two outfits – loosely defined as 'daywear' and 'evening wear' – and I photograph them in each outfit for their diptych. I just want them to wear something that is a strong reflection of themselves, and what they come up with from that basic brief is up to them.

I wasn't looking for people who just dress up at the weekend; I wanted the ones who really live their style, day in, day out. I never went to clubs to seek out potential participants and I was too shy to approach people on the street. Instead, the project expanded naturally.

There was a vintage look to the early photos, because I had a network of friends who were in that scene (this was before vintage style was commercialised). Then I started to meet friends of friends in different worlds, and from all around the world – people from Australia, China, America, Africa, across Europe. I was able to easily connect with those recommended to me via social media and show them the project – often they knew about it because their friends were part of it.

Over time, it felt like I was drawing together a creative community, creating a single tribe within which there was incredible diversity. The participants have become like my extended family… without the arguments.

The irony of what I do is that I've never been outgoing. I'd much rather be the shadow of someone rather than at the front of the party. Growing up, I never really had the confidence to interact with people. I was very shy. I didn't know how to talk to people. What do I talk about?

Maybe it would have been easier for me to just be isolated within the world of inanimate objects, photographing buildings, still-life or landscapes, but I almost forced myself to choose work where I interact with people. My height – six foot five – has been a factor as well. It's hard to remain in the shadows. People look at me when I talk about my project and say, "Are you sure you are the creator of this?" Or maybe that's just my perception.

In a magazine feature about my first *Self.Styled* exhibition in Paris in early 2016, the journalist wrote about the brooch my girlfriend made for me, and the three distinctive rings I wear on my right hand. I did some pictures for someone once and he said, "I haven't got money, but I can give you these rings." I told him: "I don't really wear rings," but accepted them as payment and since then many people have said to me, "I really like your rings." It's an ice-breaker, a talking point and there's a story connected to it. And I think a lot of people I photograph, some of whom are surprisingly shy like myself, build and build from such beginnings.

The psychological and sociological aspect of the project interests me most. We look at the surface, but the way I try to approach it is to make you think about what's below the surface. Is it who they are? Or is this how they want to project themselves? What does an individual need to give them that courage and confidence to be part of the social network, to cope with life? That's what intrigues me.

When you think about that, you move away from the idea of genres – he's a punk, she's a goth, etc. The individuals featured in this book are projecting an image and there is a deeper reason for doing that which goes beyond a trend or doing something to fit in.

It becomes very blurred between the true self and the self you project in the way you present yourself. It becomes very hard to truly be that person all the time and still be separate from it. There has to be a connection.

There was no text accompanying the diptychs in my Paris exhibition, and the viewer was invited to draw their own conclusions. This book adds another layer to the project by asking each participant to talk about their style.

To this end, I gave each person the same short list of questions as a starting point, with the proviso that it was entirely up to them how much or how little they wanted to say and to feel free to talk about whatever they wanted to. Some preferred to let their photographs do most of the talking, others wrote mini-essays or spoke at length in interviews.

I appreciated it was hard for most to talk about their style, as style is not their life, life is their style, so it is not easy to dissect what they do or don't do as it mostly comes from instinct. Almost without exception, it's clear that the people featured have an emotional link with the clothes; to them, clothes are not just pieces of fabric but associated with a memory. Style is much more than a trend; it is a link with the intimate, the identity, the unconscious.

There tends to be a focus on extremes in the *Self.Styled* project. There are a lot of performers and creatives featured in the book, and you may perceive their outfits to be outlandish. But my hope is that through the images and words, you find characteristics in them that you recognise, make a connection you might not otherwise have expected, and gain more appreciation of different ways of thinking or living.

Equally, I'm not suggesting you should dress like the people involved in the project, but perhaps you can gain more confidence to be yourself, find your own path, however that may manifest itself in what you wear. We have freedoms that others in the world don't have, and yet we conform to unwritten rules of how we're expected to be. I challenge that with *Self.Styled*.

Anthony Lycett

More

is

more

Anne-Sophie Cochevelou *Costume designer*

"I was born in Toulon in the South of France, and came to live in London to do my M.A. in Performance Design & Practice at Central Saint Martins. I feel there is more freedom to express myself in London than in Paris. Eccentric people are more visible in London than in Paris, which is known for its minimalist style.

In London, people don't stare at you in the street... as long as you queue properly. On the contrary, people come and talk to you in a friendly way, pay compliments and encourage you to look different. When you go to a party you always feel underdressed.

As a child I was really shy and introverted, expressing myself more through drawing or writing. Experiments with style came later. I think I always had a problem dealing with 'the establishment'.

I went to a very strict girls' school where everybody dressed the same. Trying to dress differently (more or less successfully) was a kind of silent rebellion. There is nothing in written law that forbids you to dress weirdly, but actually dressing up has a wonderful and underestimated power of subversion.

Costume also has the power of love – people want to touch you, to hug you. It creates a social link with people from different social backgrounds and cultures. Just by being dressed up I can go into a very select club for free (whereas I always have been a loser). You are from another world; even human law sometimes doesn't affect you anymore – being dressed up saved me from a fine for cycling on the pavement because the authorities didn't feel they had any grip on me.

I can change three or four times a day depending on the situation – job interview, working in my studio, meeting a friend, going to an exhibition, going to a party...

Dressing up is a way to control the way you want to be perceived. I feel safer being dressed up because I have total control over the information I deliver to my interlocutor. Paradoxically, by taking risks stylistically you stay safe emotionally.

Anne-Sophie Cochevelou

Where does the urge
come from to dress
the way I do?
It's the will to
aestheticise and
theatricalise my life,
a passion for colours
and unique pieces
found in flea markets
and charity shops…
and a bit of
attention-seeking."

Anne-Sophie Cochevelou

Fabulous Russella *Drag queen*

Julien Frontil *Quality assurance manager*

"When I was ten, I tried to get the local barber to shave the word 'Dannii' (Minogue) into my hair, but he refused to do it without a letter from my mum."

"The first contact is always the most important. The way a person reacts influences my behaviour: a smile or a witty comment will open dialogue, whereas a mockery or a commonplace will end the encounter."

"I don't think what I wear affects my behaviour that much. A friend of mine used to say that when I was drinking, I ruined more suits than most people have owned. I like to think that although I don't fall over as much I am still me regardless of what I wear.

I came from a working-class culture that saw dressing up as a way out of a mundane, proletarian, nine-to-five existence. It was used as a tool to hide one's poverty and was a badge of honour, an act of rebellion and an expression of the refusal to conform. I never really grew out of it. In fact I grew into it. I've always seen dressing down as the uniform of the privileged. However I am also very well aware, and so should everyone else be, that dressing down is dressing up, and is as much a vanity statement as what I choose to do. I was once asked what my greatest fear was and I answered, 'Blending in'.

Growing up I treated dressing up as a means of escape from my reality and the main reference points were, for me and a lot of other kids, the old Hollywood reruns on TV: gangster flicks, cowboy films, Elvis in the afternoon. What it was, above all, was glamorous and otherworldly. Mix that with David Bowie and Roxy Music and I was off.

My clothes are mainly vintage mid-twentieth-century classics found on my travels in my quest for the item of clothing with the perfect fit – I know it's out there. My wardrobe is supplemented by bespoke suits and made-to-measure copies of old finds. Also I like looking for good-quality bargain basics from places like M&S, Uniqlo and COS.

I wish I still owned my pink zoot suit. Probably because it reminds me of how brave I was/we were and what a risky business dressing up and standing out from the crowd was in 1980 as an 18-year-old.

What I choose to wear is a very important part of my identity, but a more playful side. If anything the way I dress has had a detrimental effect on how I am received in the art world: viewed as a dilettante, playing at art. I think I just answered whether my identity is defined by what I choose to wear."

Christos Tolera *Artist & actor*

Ewa Wilczynski *Painter*

"I approach everything in life as I would a painting composition because that's how my brain is wired, how I see the world."

"I get my clothes from all over the world.
I search high, low, far and beyond."

"If in doubt, go out."

Francois Nordmann *Vintage clothing store owner & DJ*

Princess Julia *DJ, writer, etc.*

Andie Macario *Artist, sex worker, activist & unicorn*

"My aesthetic is 'BBY Femme' (a term I have created for myself) – a hyper-queer femininity that takes all the things I hated as a child (pastel colours, pinks, ponies, unicorns, etc.) and overlapped them with a darker sexual undertone that allows me to explore my childhood trauma of sexual abuse – it provides me with a safe space to explore my understanding of my life and why I've come to be the person that I am, and to accept that.

I fought many times with my gender identity/ expression growing up. At an early age, my mother and grandmother would dress me up like a doll and I ended up looking like Shirley Temple – a look I hated and did not identify with. So when I was given a bit more freedom over my style, I became a tomboy and wore cargo pants, tank tops, etc. Then came grunge, goth and other genres which I took and mashed them all together to create my 'look'. Now my aesthetic incorporates the things I hated as a child and that feels natural because I was able to explore those things in my own time.

I have a bra from when I was 13/14 which hasn't fitted me for over ten years, but I still hold on to it as a signifier of my early adolescent sexuality. Now it holds more significance since I have become 'anti-bra'.

I've always worn what felt natural to me, despite current trends. Whilst they will somewhat feed into my wardrobe, it's not so much about the specific items, but how I make them work to my aesthetic/persona, and that for me is an organic process.

A lot of my clothes come from American Apparel (I know, *I know*), vintage shops, jumble sales, ebay, bric-a-brac shops and clothes swaps. I also have hand-me downs from my mother, aunt and friends – I love the idea of taking previously worn

Andie Macario

garments on a new journey. I also have items that were gifts from my clients as a sex worker, which is great because, you know, I get showered with gifts.

Being someone who is perceived to be a cisgendered woman means that I have to deal with sexual harassment on a daily basis (and not just within my sex work). And because of my lack of passivity (which I don't believe really exists) and my loud, assertive and strong aesthetic, it confuses people with how to confront/engage with me. More often than not, I'm seen as 'intimidating', which I've learnt to shrug off because I shouldn't have to please or bow down to anyone.

My hopes for the future? I'll be happy to just get through the day, to be honest. Also: to finally be able to leave planet Earth and return to my unicorn homeland.

I don't really care what people think of me, except that I'm a badass and not to mess with me because I'll kill you with my cuteness. But, for real, I'm like, super QT."

Andie Macario

Sophie & Polly *a.k.a.* My Bad Sister *Singers, songwriters & dancers*

Alexis Knox *Editor, creative director, celebrity fashion stylist & DJ*

"We are identical twins and have always dressed the same or similar. We have the same taste. When we were young we used to pretend to be each other and used to keep it up for as long as we could. Sometimes we'd forget which twin we were.

Interesting fact: we don't know which twin is the eldest. Mum and dad got us mixed up when we were three weeks old. So when people ask us who is the eldest we don't actually know. But we do know that the twin called Sophie was the first-born. There's only a minute in it anyway.

We have always done everything together and that's the way we like it. People ask us if it's annoying not having our own identity, but it's never bothered us at all. We love looking the same and it's totally natural for us. After all, it's more different to have an identical twin dressed the same as you."

"I like to use my wardrobe as a form of communication – what you wear says a lot about you. Or if it actually doesn't, you need to take responsibility for the fact people are likely to translate your appearance whether you like it or not. That doesn't mean I dress for other people, but it does mean that I am aware what I might wear may speak for itself. I tend to dress with colour because I am happy and confident; I never wear anything dirty or damaged, because I take care of myself and those around me as well as having a good eye for details; I also don't really like to over-complicate my clothing – I'm a no-fuss kinda person."

Jonny Woo *Performer & venue owner*

"I don't know who wrote my favourite quotation, but I saw it stuck on a friend's fridge: 'You came to NYC (insert any city/place) to be an artist, so be one.'

It was in New York in 2001 when I started going out in drag with Lavinia Co-Op and Brandon Olson with whom I started making performance art. Our drag was rebellious and a conscious middle finger to the homogenous gay scene which was so body- and style-fascist.

I don't think I am non-conformist. I have always been a performer and, when in drag, on stage or off, it's about the performance even if it's just between friends.

Drag is more outré and in drag you can't help but be more OTT. I'm borderline transvestite and borderline drag queen. I actually really like a lot of the women's clothes I choose to wear, although they are not really designed for regular women, so I inhabit a fantasy but it's not real life for me.

My boy clothes have always been more reserved. They come from a mix of vintage and the high street although the cut of a lot of stores is for skinny twentysomethings. I can't wait for 'skinny' as a trend to be over.

My favourite drag pieces tend to be made by friends, I have an ever-growing collection of kaftans by a variety of designers including Julian J. Smith who cuts a wonderful shape every time.

The drag is an extension of my feminine personae and affords me the ability to wear all the amazing styles and looks usually only available to women. I love so many women's clothes, I'm very lucky to be able to enjoy both and indulge my Seventies suburban sartorial fantasies, but it's not real life for me.

I am pretty conservative in the day and like to blend. I like to feel part of the bigger society. I am comfortable with that. In the day, I think I like my clothes to show an element of togetherness and confidence. I have had long periods in my life which have been chaos; whilst at times exciting, it can also be devastating.

Jonny Woo

In the past drag was
a confrontation
and expressed rebellion.
Then it became very much
a part of my creativity
and now it is more
indulgence. As a man,
I am enjoying growing
into my style and accepting
who I am. I think my style
is very English and I dress
for myself and to make
myself feel good."

Jonny Woo

Charles Adesanya *Fashion stylist*

"Your identity is defined by your human character, who you are as a person,
be it kind, generous, smart. Clothing is a fun method of self-expression
but does not define my personal identity or *vice versa*."

"I grew up in a very working-class, big family and was actually pretty shy. I was desperately trying to pretend to be straight so was 'dressing up' in a different way: bootcut jeans, Ben Sherman shirts and Reebok Classics.

I always ask myself: 'Are you happy today?' If I am not I do something to change it. Life is short."

"My aim as a cisgendered drag queen is for people to question the constructed categories of gender and especially femininity and feminine beauty in culture.

In future, I hope to become a bigger and better drag queen, to have a community of people around me who inspire me and each other to be better versions of ourselves and openly challenge standards of representation."

Glyn Fussell *Party organiser & owner of a creative agency & TV company*

Victoria Sin *Artist, drag queen, illustrator, etc.*

Duggie Fields *Artist*

"Visiting the USA for the first time in 1968 was an eye-opener as to how people responded to me. Earlier, at the start of London's tourist boom, I had gotten used to American tourists asking to take my photo out in the street with 'Gee, you look so cute'.

In New York, though, having gone only armed with a couple of phone numbers, nowhere to stay, little money and a companion (though soon on my own), I found myself being welcomed into homes, parties, events and clubs because of the way I looked, and even followed in the street.

On the subway I had a group of Hell's Angels who were storming through the carriage come sit next to me and shake my hand. On the other hand, the drivers in a five-lane highway full of slow-moving, rush-hour traffic in Kansas City screamed abuse and jeered at me. Terrifying – and I thought I'd especially dressed in my blandest clothes.

Around the turn of the Seventies, I started being photographed more for my work and later for my home, than for just the way I looked. But for me these were all aspects of visual expression, visual communication, the visual world, where everything interacts. Somehow I always felt I couldn't apply myself to the strict confines of a flat picture-plane canvas unless I thought about the context of what was around it, and apply myself to that also. Of course that was not always possible in temporary, rented, shared homes and college studios. The canvas that was always available though was the self. Never thought what I was doing was making art outside of the canvas and for years I only identified myself as a painter.

The mid-Seventies saw my world described in print as a *Gesamtkunstwerk*. Photographs with my paintings and home appeared frequently in international publications as my evolving way of self-presentation coalesced into a look with simple elements: eyebrows and curl, basically, a look that has become recognisable as 'mine' almost ever since.

My sense of self it seems has imposed a structure on my behaviour and appearance and its interaction in the outside world.

Duggie Fields

This self is a minimal creation. It occurs daily as part of a morning ritual, a way of focusing on the day, as automatic now as brushing my teeth, taking no time and no thought.

Putting clothes on relates
partially to the climate, and in
part to the feeling of the moment.
Can be the same from day to day.
Can demand fresh choice.
Can be satisfied instantly,
followed by infrequent periods
of time-consuming, irrational
rejection and angst.

Change is frequently desired,
and yet the same things can satisfy
constantly for days, years or even
decades. Often nothing to do with
whether I am going out the door
anywhere or not, or expecting
visitors home or not.

Taste remains constant,
and constantly changing.
Reactions are curious, from
the complimentary to the abusive,
sometimes extremes of both.

I get my clothes from anywhere: chain stores, charity shops, street markets, ebay, car-boots, designers and tailors who make things for me, things that I get given. Sales. I enjoy change, but end up wearing the same things continuously at the same time. Guess there is an evolution over time around certain recurring themes, but I don't like having to look for specific items, preferring chance encounters of the eyes, and things that push the boundaries of my taste.

Currently, the items of clothing that mean most to me are a new pair of all-white trainers. For maybe the last 40 years, almost continuously, I've wanted to see all-white when I look down at my feet, between me and the ground, whatever the shoe. These are the most comfortable possibly ever, and that's been the next most important thing that shoes have had to be for me. They are sort of like having a visual platform that separates me from the world around. Until I step into a puddle, that is."

Duggie Fields

Fred Butler *Accessories designer*

"Breakfast for me is Weetabix,
and tea in a rainbow mug."

Something fresh, raw & filling, but no set menu

Immodesty Blaize *Burlesque performer, artist & author*

"What is our identity and character other than what mood we're in? Who I am, not what I do, defines what I choose to wear.

People's expectations may be that a burlesque dancer should be wearing victory rolls, red lipstick and a Fifties pinup dress. This to me is a form of style convention; why do I need to wear this uniform to advertise one aspect of my job?

I wear things to feel comfortable in my skin, things that enhance my shape, and work with my character – I want to wear my clothes, not for my clothes to wear me. If a masculine-tailored tuxedo and turban makes me feel va-va-voom on a certain day, then that's what I'll wear. Or maybe I'll feel like facing the world with big hair and swinging hips. I go with my mood, as style to me comes from authenticity.

I just like to feel vampy and strong, ready to get down to business and get shit done. I also love hats with a passion. In another lifetime I'm sure I'd have been a milliner.

I was simply never fashionable. As a teenager in the Nineties there were lots of ugly commercial fashions that looked terrible on me – big baggy jeans, wallabee shoes, cargo pants, puffa jackets. None of it worked on my shape or made me feel good, so like flinging a life-raft out into the ocean and jumping ship, I desperately tried to find things that wouldn't make me look like the Michelin Man and things that would make me feel a bit more glamorous.

Immodesty Blaize

I'd scour charity shops for furs and scarves that looking back, made me look like I was auditioning for *Grey Gardens*. I made so many cringeworthy fashion mistakes in my quest but I didn't really care.

I was looking up to style icons like Grace Jones, Jean-Paul Gaultier on *Eurotrash*, Vivienne Westwood twirling in no knickers at Buckingham Palace, Madonna in pointy bras, Alexis Colby in *Dynasty*. Before I got into Italian Cinecitta movies and my retro idols, these were the people on my TV screen and in the newspapers having fun with their fashion and that's where I wanted to be, rather than spending my pocket money on the right Fila trainers to fit in, or flashing Ralph Lauren logos everywhere.

As Tom Ford says, dressing well is a form of good manners; I continue that respect when interacting with people. But what people think of me when they see me is none of my business.

I dress for myself. I wore my nails long and sharp for about ten years and I was often told they made me unapproachable, but the first time my husband set eyes on me he noticed me tapping my blood-red sharp claws impatiently on the bar. He was intrigued immediately, and now we're married. Whether for work or leisure, if you dress as yourself, for yourself, the right people for you come into your world."

Immodesty Blaize

Andrew Logan *Sculptor*

"My favourite saying: 'If you have a penny, spend half on bread to live, and half on a rose for the reason for living.'"

Robert Wilde-Evans *Retail assistant for a classic British shoe- & boot-making company*

"I identify myself as a gentleman with a traditional – but not necessarily stuffy – outlook on life. I enjoy wearing tweed jackets, colourful trousers, hats, good shoes, etc., not because I think it's what I should be wearing but because it's what I want to wear. People may identify me as a very conservative individual based on the way I dress whereas, in fact, I'm really rather liberal. Identity helps one choose what to wear, but I'm not certain it defines it in black-and-white certainty.

I suppose I really just have an urge to be comfortable in myself, to dress as I like, not to put on a show for others, but to make myself happy – because life's too short to be miserable. Of course, dressing as I do isn't necessarily cheap and I hasten to add that I do not devote my life purely to maintaining an exceptional standard of dress, but I do it because, well, what's the point in not doing it?

I don't believe I have ever put on affected mannerisms or attitudes based on the way I dress – that would be rather false and shallow; to pretend to be something I am not. I am who I am, but dressing well helps to give me the confidence to talk to all sorts of people and has certainly helped me to get along in life in all sorts of ways and situations far too numerous to recall here.

I know for a fact that many people have had pre-conceived ideas about me – that I went to a public school because of my accent; that I must lead a privileged life because of the way I talk and the way I dress. I rather enjoy letting them think that, proving them wrong, or indeed being a slight enigma.

First and foremost, I'd like people to immediately think of me as a gentleman – the classic British stereotype perhaps, but there's no harm in that. I would hope they'd see a smartly dressed, interesting-looking man who perhaps has a story or two to tell, but also that there's something about him impossible to quite pinpoint: is he rich or poor? Local or just visiting? How old is he? What has life brought his way? I, of course, wouldn't be so complacent as to think I was worth talking about, but if I were it makes me smile to think I could be a subject of interest to someone."

Bethan Laura Wood *Designer & artist*

"I am normally a very good acid test of whether you should get a clown in
or not for a small child's birthday party. If they stare and smile at me,
get one; if they cry and run away, maybe wait a few years."

"4 somethin lost there iz somethin found
i lost my culture but i found a POund."

"I love colour, cartoons, drag, glitter, clashing
prints and being as silly as possible."

Adio West *ELeGant Noize makeR*

Amy Redmond *a.k.a.* Amy Zing *Party organiser*

Mark Powell *Tailor*

"I first got jackets tailored for myself at age 12, 13. Tailors were in every suburban high street back then and my dad was working in textiles so I could get fabric from him.

My dad was very much of the old school where the guy would go to the tailor's and have a suit made. And my mum worked as a dresser in the theatre for Charles Fox's company – Fox was a famous costumier in the Thirties and Forties. It's only in the last ten years or so doing interviews about my work that I've realised these factors must have had an influence on me. At the time, I just did it – I knew the style I wanted and asked the tailor to make it for me.

I went through all the usual sub-cultures when I was a kid. I was a bit too young to be a first-generation skinhead, but I was certainly a suedehead from 1971 onwards. I suppose the first time I started to express myself more as an individual was the soul-boy era, around 1975, '76. There was a lot of influence from people like David Bowie, Bryan Ferry as well – I got the Bowie *Pin Ups* suit look when I was about 15. You could only buy flares in the shops at that time unless you went to a second-hand shop, so they were the first pair of trousers I made myself. Started pretty young.

I had my first shop by the time I was 24, in 1985, and my whole thing from the start was using tailoring as a way to express individual style, as the mods, skinheads, teddy boys and most of the sub-cultures did, rather than just using tailoring to look smart or elegant.

I've got a big thing for coats. I've got some amazing coats I've designed and made over the years. Coats can be useful because you can always throw them over the top when you're not particularly dressed up.

There's one really lovely 1930s-style overcoat which we do ready-to-wear in the shop – I've got four of them – and an Edwardian-influenced coat, or a nice, short peacoat (which I'm wearing in my daywear photo) which looks quite contemporary. In fact, a lot of the clothes

Mark Powell

I do these days, I don't really draw back to nostalgia because everyone's trying to do the vintage thing. Guys in hats, waistcoats and watchchains have suddenly become quite fashionable – I've been doing that for 35, 40 years.

I think you've got to get the balance between vintage and modern. In my early days, I would have done a Fifties, Sixties or Seventies look in a purer way, but over the years, I've managed to take all these eclectic influences to create my own style.

You see fashionistas and they are trying so hard. Fashion Week in London has become so ridiculous, more about people who come dressed almost like Christmas trees. Look at the great designers like Chanel; it was about their own style that then extended into their clothing. All the great style icons look at ease in what they wear, as if it's effortless.

Men's tailoring is having a renaissance, because everything got so casual. Guys are not just wearing a suit for the office, but for style and fashion. Although I do think a lot of the modern tailoring is a little generic, formulaic. Whether it's Daniel Craig or Tom Hardy on the red carpet, they all look much the same – that over-tailored look with arms bursting out the seams and chest pulling on the buttons.

Years ago if you wanted to create a look, you might look at some books or magazines to do some research, you couldn't just google it. The internet can contribute to a lack of individuality in some ways.

I learnt from an early age how dressing up can empower you and that's never changed. The way you dress does affect the way you are perceived, certainly. I remember coming out of the Carlyle Hotel in New York all dressed up, getting in the cab, and the driver saying to me: 'Are you a prince?' ... 'If I open my mouth, mate, you know I ain't!'"

Mark Powell

Sorrel Mocchia di Coggiola *Portrait painter & organiser of art-related events*

"I must have been six or seven when my grandmother gave me a trunk of old clothes for playing dress-up: scarves and weird hats with huge flowers on them and Seventies lace nightgowns. It was heaven. I suppose I haven't really changed since then.

On my first trip to Paris at age 11, I insisted that everyone at a dinner party wear turbans and veils.

Looking a bit odd is not a bad way to filter out the fools. It also allows shy people to pass as aloof and eccentric, then cures them of their shyness as they have to come to their own defence. This was the case with me.

I dress the way I do because it's how I feel comfortable. Being stared at in the street is an unfortunate side-effect, which is why I never wear glasses.

When people see me I'd rather they didn't think about me too hard… only I do think it's sweet when people stop to tell me that I remind them (fondly) of a long-lost grandmother."

Kala Kala *Multidisciplinary artist*

"I feel there's an indication
and possibility of my
clothes being an outward
representation of my inner soul,
my feelings regarding beautiful
nature, this wonderful life
and colourful planet.
My inner thoughts are
a more strongly beautiful way
of connecting from inner
realisation to the outer beautiful
planet and divine light.

Kala Kala

My profession is loving life and living in arts such as singing, writing, dancing, abstract art forms, painting and developing new styles of fashion. Everyday I discover new art forms.

I never even dreamed about not conforming in society when I was young, not until October 2010 when I started to awaken and this transformation and spiritual realisation began. Still I feel that I am in a continuous process of further awakening.

I have collected most of my clothing from India and the UK, especially Greater London. I have found items from the streets of London, lots of temples, lots of charity shops, and sometimes I have been gifted items by the beautiful golden diamond soul, Daniel Lismore [see page 190]. I don't really have a favourite item as they are all colourful and beautiful but I see the turban as a crown gifted by the almighty.

I feel that God is gifting me all these wonderful items because many items are waiting for me to be collected and through these items I feel I am connecting to the Lord, nature and great souls.

Feeling the unconditional love from people, objects and nature makes me feel blessed, and I feel the divine light talking to me through anything. The universe is infinite and all its contents are limitless, just like unconditional love. I feel the colour and clothing I wear is more effective in connecting with beautiful souls, but with regards to nature and the divine light, it is not necessarily important to wear any particular type of clothing. We are all colourful souls, that's why we are all being affected by the colours around us.

It never crosses my mind what others think about my appearance, but I always wish the best for everyone whether I meet them or not and I wish for them to think in a beautiful way for themselves.

I want to keep loving life deeply, highly, and around me everywhere until every last breath of this human skinsuit. I also hope that others will experience what I am experiencing with God's blessings, and the world will be a more humble, kind, wonderful and colourful place. This is the truth to achieving free spirituality."

Kala Kala

Natty Bo *Artist, singer, performer & DJ*

Lady Gonzalez *Fashion designer, stylist & visual artist*

"The music I listened to reflected my style. As a teen it was rebel music and I identified with outcasts, freaks, original stylers and mainly anyone who accepted me for who I was.

Then there was my punk-dada-surreal side: I wore attachments like a telephone round my neck; sometimes suits on backwards with a shop sign hanging round my neck; or PJs with hobnail boots… I even wore a TV screen... this became more acceptable when I was performing in Archaos Circus.

Jamaican music was a huge influence apart from singing and writing ska and rocksteady. I had dreads when I was 20, 21. I wore huge hats, beaver hats, 8 piece caps, Pierrot feather hats and some other invented concoctions which I thought made really good silhouettes."

"I remember clearly me and my teenage best-friend-forever were sitting in the roof of my house at 13 years old, smoking what was probably one of our first-ever spliffs. We promised each other that from that point on we would never dress like anyone else and were gonna create our own complete style. And we did. From then on we made our own clothes, glueing and safety-pinning and completely DIY-ing our style with no knowledge of clothes construction, but a lot of eagerness to be loud and bold. We triggered a sort of movement in our town and soon we were about ten girls going to a pretty conservative school looking like we had come out of a Japanese street-style magazine.

When people see me, I hope they think, 'Look at that hot piece of a fun lady. Perhaps I should remember to take life with a pinch of technicoloured salt.'"

Dame Zandra Rhodes *Textile, dress & opera designer*

"I dress to represent
myself, my clothes, my
prints and what I believe
in. I am always selling
myself and my brand.
If I did not wear my own
clothes it would mean
I did not believe in them.
I try to design clothes
that I personally covet
and want to wear. If I don't
wear and believe in what
I design, who else will?

Dame Zandra Rhodes

My clothes are all from my own design collection. It's important to represent my own work. Otherwise, why do I design?

Right from my final year in college in 1964, I had developed my own distinctive make-up and hair looks to go with my clothes. I started to develop my style soon after leaving the Royal College of Art textile school, but probably came totally into my own from 1969, when I created my own collection, which I wore myself, with special make-up.

Long before that, there were signs of being a non-conformist. I would wear things from my mother's dress shows at the college where she taught and didn't care if other children made fun of me – like on Sundays when I ran through the park so the other children didn't laugh at me and throw stones.

When people see me wearing my clothes, I hope that they like what they see, that they can identify with them and would like to wear them too.

So many of my clothes tell their own story. Whether they are fronds cut around the print and then with feathers on the ends, or holes in jersey with jewelled safety pins. My punk wedding dress is enshrined in glory at the Met Museum New York.

I hope that my work will have made a memorable and original contribution to the history of fashion and printed textile imagery.

My favourite saying is: 'Good, better, best. Never let it rest. Till your good is better and your better is best.'"

Dame Zandra Rhodes

"I've always done my own thing, living in my own 'Gaffy's world'. I had a strict upbringing so I was the ultimate rebel. I always did the opposite of what I was supposed to do. Some of my earliest memories are sitting in the 'naughty corner' (the strawberry patch) in kindergarten at the age of four.

I dress how I feel and colour makes me feel high like a drug; it gives me energy and life.

What I wear is an expression of my creativity. I have a lot of fun with it. I'm influenced and inspired by colour and traditional threads I collect on my travels so I love mixing and matching them all.

I would like people not to think too much when they see me. I would prefer them to smile and enjoy the rainbow feasted upon their eyes."

"I used to be obsessed with girly transfer tattoos and anything sparkly; I kind of haven't changed. I've always been a firm believer in colour therapy. I think print and vibrant colours can easily lift your spirits. I want to come across as a happy and confident person and I hope that's what my style conveys. And if it makes a few other people smile on the way then that's just a bonus."

Gaffy Gaffiero *Performer & DJ*

Byron London *Full-time fabulous, soon-to-be student of prosthetic make-up*

Bishi Bhattacharya *Musician, artist, multimedia performer, DJ, etc.*

"I think dressing and glamour are a tonic to life's darkness, which is in abundance. Clothes are expression and a release. Dressing differently comes with ridicule and abuse, but as long as you own it, you hold the keys."

Rosy Pendlebury *Art historian, performer, event manager & producer*

"The way I dress depends on how I'm feeling, how I'd like to be feeling, the people around me, where I'm going, what I'm doing... How you're dressed can be powerfully transformative both for you, other people and the space around you.

I think dressing differently invites interaction with people, which is something I welcome. It gives them a reason to talk to you and that's positive so much more often than it isn't. I saw the most wonderful older lady on a train a couple of weeks ago who had pink hair and was wearing a leopard-print coat similar to mine and we caught each other's eyes and waved and then I went over to sit with and talk to her. Her name was Anne, she was 84 years old and on her way home from a hospital appointment and we talked all the way to my stop and then hugged and said goodbye. If we hadn't both been dressed differently but similarly, we'd have missed out on a really uplifting moment of connection with a stranger.

I've currently got pink hair and one of my favourite things in the world is the daily awe-struck gawps and comments from little girls on the street, or the tube or the checkout queue. The mum whose sleeve they're tugging on might not thank me for it now, but I love planting the idea in my mini sisters' heads that they don't have to fit in, that they can express themselves creatively, and that their hair, bodies and style are something they have ownership of."

Live solely & utterly in each rewarding moment of every day

Molly Parkin *Writer & artist*

"I was born (3 February 1932) into a Welsh-speaking household on the side of a wild and wonderfully inspirational mountain in a Welsh coal-mining village community, Pontycymmer, Garw Valley, in South Wales.

My parents moved to London with limited funds, to the seediest of shabby suburbs, but war broke out in 1939 and I was rescued from the depression of my mundane surroundings when I was evacuated back to my Welsh valley to live with my maternal grandparents. There my artistic abilities blossomed, painting the mountains on my own from the age of seven, but at that same age, I discovered the solitary joy in the heavenly art of dressing up in front of a full-length mirror, secretly donning the splendour of my granny's 1920s finery stowed away in her boxroom.

Returning home at the end of the war, London took on a different slant when my parents moved to running a small hotel in Paddington, a walk away from the fashion shops of the West End. Liberty's inspired me more than the rest, and it was here, later, in the Fifties, that Mr Liberty himself featured my vast abstract impressionist landscapes in the Regent Street windows after I left art school and painted professionally. London had become a showcase for me artistically, although I was still years away from achieving the status of 'fashion icon' and the undisputed queen of Bohemia.

Self-expression is as much a character trait as kindness, generosity, spirituality, self-belief. I came from a family of beautiful womenfolk who instinctively dressed with an innate sense of style. People called it a flair. I inherited this (and colour sense) so I always stood out in a crowd. As a schoolgirl I would be the only one at the bus stop after school still wearing my school hat. But with the brim turned down, low over my fringe, and the collars of my school uniform blouse and blazer turned up. And the belt of my gymslip worn low on the hip. I sensed how to transform a mundane uniform into a personal statement.

Molly Parkin

I was always a rule-breaker, curious to test the water, to defy authority, to challenge the norm. A typical Aquarian. It was never a ruse to attract attention, simply a need to shake up the proceedings and introduce life and change and lightheartedness.

Everybody's identity defines what they choose to wear. Mine varies, dependent on my moods, my outlook at any given hour of the day or night. I can wake up and choose an all-black evening ensemble: jet jewellery, a black sequin shoulder shrug, sooty sweeping chiffon skirts, an ebony velvet cloche on my head… and eat my breakfast in my garden, beneath a vast (black) umbrella if it's raining of course.

Then I certainly undergo various outfits during the day. Clothes, for me, are as much a pastime as any other. That's why I now make all my own clothes – for the vast variety.

I am in essence a loner – all artists are. The clothes, the outfits, are a secondary aspect for me, simply the hurling together of shapes and colours. The end result and the effect it has on others is of the least importance.

I apply the same principles as the approach to covering a canvas with paint and shapes and an enduring image. I treasure that completed work of art.

My appearance may be captured in the countless photographs printed of me, but they don't touch my soul in the same way as the art, or as one of my own pieces of poetry."

Molly Parkin

"I grew up in a heavily narrow-minded area. I always had a desire to wear eccentric and more outlandish clothing, but the feeling that I had to fit in pretty much subdued sartorial aspirations, until my mid-twenties where my style slowly started to organically flourish.

I was 27 years old and dealing with the overwhelming stress of worrying about what other people thought about me, when I had an epiphany that it is actually futile to do so, as you can not control people's thoughts. Better to be free of them completely and express yourself as you desire."

"Once I went to the local supermarket wearing 'normal' clothes – i.e. a long cardigan and my running shoes – as I urgently needed some food. A man ran up to me and said: 'Oh my God, are you okay?'

I said, 'Yes, I'm fine, what do you mean?' 'You're not dressed in your usual garb. I thought something had happened.' Needless to say, I won't have another day off again."

Sane Phoenix *Graphic designer*

Annette Bette Kellow *Actress, writer & vintage model*

Nadia Lee Cohen *Photographer, film-maker & image-maker*

"I want a Wikipedia page – it's all I really care about in this world.
What would I like people to think about me when they see me in the street?
That's the girl from Wikipedia."

Albion Geovictwardian *Freelance legal, creative & business consultant*

"For breakfast, I eat Imperial Muesli (my own blend) with oat milk and Scottish Heather Honey accompanied by strongly brewed English Breakfast Tea. 'Imperial' because it contains ingredients from the countries which made up The British Empire. A nod to George Orwell is contained in the name.

The harmony of proportion in Geovictwardian style is based upon the Classical School of architecture, which is rooted in the proportions of a human body, thus providing a template for top-to-toe balance.

My grey herringbone Tweed Norfolk jacket typifies the ethos of Geovictwardianism being practical and elegant. Designed for strength, versatility and to maintain its appearance in inclement weather, it is a modern classic.

Unquestionably, my garments reflect an inner approach to life. Putting on a full set of smart clothes (especially a collar and tie or stock) causes an erect posture and more elegant speech. Others perceive this aura and offer (usually) more respect than a casual appearance elicits from them. However, sometimes a street urchin will call me a 'posh geezer' and London taxi drivers call out 'Sherlock Holmes'. A small child once asked me if I was William Morris, when I was on a train going through Walthamstow. Another time it was 'Scarlet Pimpernel' from a teenager.

An odd tale of toggery: I was invited to one of the gentlemen's clubs in St James's in London's West End and I was wearing a stock, red velvet waistcoat, double-breasted blue velvet jacket, red corduroy trousers and black tassel loafers. At the door I was asked to remove the stock and put on a tie, otherwise I would not be allowed entry, even though the stock pre-dates the tie as an item of neckwear and the club dated back to the time when men wore stocks.

At a bar in Islington, North London, I was refused a drink and required to leave because I was wearing 'office attire' and the bar had a dress code of 'no office attire'. I was wearing the same clothes as when I was refused entry to the St James's club.

When people see me, I'd like them to think that either they have seen a ghost from the Georgian, Victorian or Edwardian periods or that they have seen someone who is outside of the current system – a genuine independent.

My hope is that one day we will all return to our true home. An esoteric, mystical wish steeped in Paganism. We are all on a colossal journey which will take us full circle until we reach the point where we began. Everyone goes home: there are no failures.

Putting on certain garments causes a change in a person, called 'The Transformation'. It is the same as when a superhero like Batman or Superman changes from ordinary clothes to their special outfit: the mind alters at the same time, following which conduct changes and ability is enhanced. This can bring about revolutions if allowed to run free, as all dress should be liberating both for the wearer and for the observer."

Albion Geovictwardian

Annika Caswell *Actress & bespoke tailor*

"When I was 16, I developed a deep love for television period dramas, and didn't understand why I shouldn't be able to dress from those eras. And so I went to antique fairs and found corsets, petticoats, skirts, dresses and shoes, and re-enacted my favourite scenes on my own on the Quantock Hills in Somerset. I must have been quite a sight driving my mother's gold Ford Fiesta wearing a corset and Victorian gown. I didn't care about anyone in the world then. I already felt so different to anyone else I knew.

I remember the first time I stayed up all night to do my GCSE coursework. At 6am I dressed in my full Victorian corsets, petticoats, gown and boots, and ran across the fields outside my village as the sun came up. I think I was celebrating by pretending to be Catherine from *Wuthering Heights*.

I guess I've always been a frustrated actress — something I was always too shy to follow as a young girl. So when I dress myself each day it is to suit the character I most feel like I am inhabiting that day.

The way I dress makes me feel like a lady. I'm naturally incredibly shy, and so my clothes are also a veneer that I feel protected by. People treat me as I love to be treated when I am properly dressed, and I feel confident and theatrical, expressive and free.

From my private collection, the piece I am wearing in my evening wear photo means the most to me. It is a mustard silk jersey couture gown from the late 1930s. It has no label, so I have always secretly hoped it is a Schiaparelli sample because of the huge buttons and extravagant embroidery.

But on a purely personal level, after my father's death, his garage overalls have become the most precious garment I own. He wore them when he painstakingly restored our Triumph Herald."

Nathan French *Artist*

"I have never conformed."

Rubyyy Jones *Performer, producer & artist*

Holly-Ann Buck *a.k.a.* Collagism *2D, 3D & audio-visual collagist*

Anna Swiczeniuk *Lingerie brand manager, DJ & photographer*

Mikey Woodbridge *Musician, songwriter, etc.*

"I just directed my first play, a queer version of *The Little Prince*, and I love the line: 'What is visible to the eye isn't what's important. It is what one sees with one's heart that is truly special.'

The big red coat I'm wearing in my evening wear photo has been around the world with me. She's so much my onstage persona, I bought another in baby blue for when I'm feeling coquettish as opposed to devastating."

Rubyyy Jones

"My handbag (in my evening wear photo) was a gift from a great friend. I can change the collage to match with my outfit. I use it as my everyday bag even though it's completely impractical and barely fits my keys, lipstick and mobile. It's filled with love; literally lined with my friend's childhood stamp collection. I love it because it means she's always with me. I'm a total sentimentalist – I have few possessions but cherish various trinkets from the people I love."

Holly-Ann Buck *a.k.a.* Collagism

"My surname was my Ukrainian grand-father's. He supposedly escaped the Red Army by holding onto the bottom of a train.

My natural state is intimidating. Something that's only partly an assumption of the onlooker, and partly a coping mechanism for being a female in a large city. The way I dress isn't inviting, which isn't to say I won't be friendly should someone strike up a conversation. It gives me confidence, but the world is a terrifying place, and I don't delude myself by dressing as if it isn't. The way I dress is, in many ways, armour."

Anna Swiczeniuk

"I always found the pieces that I make or customise myself to be my favourite. Something about it coming from my inner core, creativity and vision, and then wearing that upon my external self makes me feel sexy and beyond, no matter how ugly someone else may find the piece.

When I'm fully dressed up and in full make-up I definitely have more confidence and feel like I can talk to people and open up more because I feel like I am presenting myself as the best person I can be. So therefore I'm happier, I can think more clearly and give all of myself to people."

Mikey Woodbridge

Joshua Kane *Fashion house owner & managing director*

"I was always drawing and designing things when I was young. My mother was an interior designer, and she ran her design office from our house. So for as long as I can remember, I was 'in design' in one way or another.

When I was 16 and 17 I began experimenting with clothing. I went out to shops and was unable to find any clothes that I liked, so I started customising old clothes, finding ways to make them more unique and more how I wanted them to look. That was the birth of the obsession.

Rather than identity defining what I choose to wear, it's self-expression. It's my own series of ways in which I choose to express myself and goes some way to define who I am. But I'm a bit of a chameleon. In the morning, I ride into the office on my skateboard with a T-shirt, jeans and a hat. Half an hour later, I'm in a three-piece suit and look like a completely different person. But I love both of those aesthetics equally.

Self-expression is vital to every human being, otherwise we become caged rats. And if we are unable to express ourselves, we become repressed and repressed people are never happy.

There is definitely a relationship between the way I present myself and the way I interact with people; one definitely influences the other. When you put on a really well-fitted suit and you look at yourself in the mirror and you change your posture and feel good about yourself, you might not know technically why you feel good, but you do. That then affects the way you talk. If you feel confident, that you look good, you will act more confidently. It's human nature.

I don't really care what people think about me if they see me in the street, though. I would like to think that someone could appreciate it at some level, whether they love it or hate it, but gaining approval is certainly not my benchmark.

I wear my own clothes – the whole wardrobe: suits, shirts, shoes, socks, coats,

Joshua Kane

bags, umbrellas… everything. So it would be pretty nonsensical to wear someone else's.

My favourite item is a red leather bomber jacket with lambswool fur and big gold zips, probably because it was something I really enjoyed designing and also because I'm known for my tailoring. Designing with leather – outerwear, coats, etc. – is something I've done a huge amount before in previous companies and it was fun to do it under my own guise. It felt like two fingers up at the past.

I don't have one single mantra I live by… I have many. They are more benchmarks than anything else. There was a wonderful quote – I think it was by Cary Grant – 'You can tell the quality of a gentleman by what he wears on his feet and his wrist,' referencing that even on people's most casual days, a good pair of shoes and a half-decent watch is a staple of someone who has some form of sartorial correctness. That's something I always like to have in the back of my mind, especially as we meet all manner of individuals from all walks of life every day.

Obviously, never judging people by what they are wearing is really important, but it's nice that some people will make an effort."

Joshua Kane

Sorapol *Fashion designer*

"Fashion is a beautiful kind of pain."

"As a child, my nickname was simply 'weirdo' to my friends and family, so I guess there was probably something a bit out of the ordinary about me.

I was at an all-girls high school. I was the only one sporting half-shaved blue-and-green hair with garish neon nose studs. Nobody ever criticised my style though – I think the other girls respected my decision to be different. Or maybe they were just scared.

Apparently as a child I wanted to be a lollipop lady because it meant that I could work very few hours and dress up in fluorescent costume everyday. In a way I pretty much achieved that dream by becoming a full-time performer – plus the outfits are much more glamorous. So I guess my life goals have been achieved; now it's time to start planning new ones.

I have always been a very shy, moody and introverted person, but with a very creative and theatrical flair, so I think that unconsciously my personality traits are definitely reflected in my style. And I am almost always hiding behind a hat. I have an unhealthy obsession with hats – they are quite literally taking over my life."

Charlotte VKA *International performer, etc.*

David Carter *Interior designer, hotelier & purveyor of whimsical magical experiences*

"Clothes should ideally be an expression of who we are, providing a little window on to our inner lives, but most people choose, or are sometimes obliged, to wear a 'uniform' and prefer to simply blend in.

Of course, this doesn't mean that just because someone dresses in an uninteresting way they are not going to be witty, charming and intelligent.

It is sadly often the case that some of the most stylish looking people are actually incredibly dull – all plumage and no personality.

'Fashion' is something anyone can simply buy in a shop, and even 'style' can be acquired with the help of the right personal shopper or stylist. The adage that you should never judge a book by its cover applies equally to clothes. Obviously in my case, we have the perfect marriage of sparkling personality and effortless style."

Twinks Burnett *Fashion stylist*

"I attended a military school for the entirety of my teens. When allowed to express myself, I just went a little over the top. I was never very good at being told to fall into line. Colour is my expression."

Always

different

&

always

a lot

Jenkin Van Zyl *Film-maker & sculptor*

"Forces of the occult beyond my control define what I choose to wear. I think I was dropped on the floor during my birth or something. There were early signs of non-conforming, such as rifling through my mum's make-up cabinet and wardrobe to transform into a middle-aged South African woman."

"I am a curve model and I don't listen to the media's standards of what I should wear for my body type. I hope I give confidence to all the young girls to wear what they want, although I'm sure some people think I'm too much – not that I care, though.

I bought the green sequin dress in a vintage store: it is handmade and completely one of a kind. Shortly after the image was first published I was contacted by Amy Griffith, the California-born owner of Eaton House Studio, the luxury guest house in Essex, England, who knew that her mother had a very similar dress in the Eighties which was also handmade. I did some research and we realised it was the same dress; it had travelled overseas and ended up in this store. Since then myself and Amy have become soul sistas!"

Felicity Hayward *Model & artist*

Gustav Temple *Magazine editor*

"Around the time I turned 35, I realised I could not possibly continue dressing like a young person, so I delved deeply into the fashion choices for men from the past when they reached the beginning of middle age. There seemed to be something dignified, and even dandified, about accepting the passing years and adapting one's wardrobe to them. Thus *The Chap* magazine was born out of such investigations.

In a sense my dress code, like most chaps, is a sort of conformity, or at least was once. By today's standards, dressing like a 1940s English gentleman is actually quite radical, so I suppose this fitted in with the version of non-conformity I had adopted as a youth, when I wore frilly dandy shirts, top hats and frock coats.

I don't think identity defines what you choose to wear. Not in the slightest. I think clothes expand from one's sense of who one is, and this can change daily. What defines what I choose to wear is how I feel when I get up in the morning. On some days that might mean simply staying in pyjamas, dressing gown and slippers all day (though these items are just as carefully sourced as all other daywear).

I dress as I do from a desire to look stylish, different, elegant and dandyish all the time. A desire not to be taken for just another bloke on the high street in cargo pants and a hoodie, trying to blend in with all the others. My wish is that every last pair of trainers, baseball caps and hooded tops be wiped off the face of the Earth, and replaced by brogues, trilbies and tweed jackets.

As Jeeves once replied to Wooster when asked, 'What do ties matter, Jeeves, at a time like this?' 'There are no occasions when ties do not matter, sir.'

When dressed properly, one tends to be more polite to people, as it would look odd if one went around shouting at folk while wearing a three-piece suit and a fedora.

I'd like people who see me in the street to think: 'I say, there goes a fabulously dressed cove! He looks like he leads an interesting life and doesn't take any balderdash from anybody.'

Gustav Temple

All the clothes I own mean a lot to me… I suppose I am very attached to an original 1940s brown pinstripe demob suit, on account of its chequered history and how rare such items are – especially when they fit you. I've also got a top hat which is rather nice, but every time I wear it I seem to end up married, so I've decided to chuck it away."

Gustav Temple

George Bourgeois *Genderblind singing clown*

"My favourite item of clothing aged four was a pair of bubblegum-pink glittery leggings, which I think belonged to my sister. My mother would try to bribe me not to wear them out of the house, but it never worked. I wore them with a polka dot cape and a Mickey Mouse jumper and it's still one of my favourite outfits.

I had a very confused style throughout my teens. I'd try to adopt the uniform of different groups and then hated it as soon as I fitted in. Whichever sub-group style I tried – goth, skater, sporty – as soon as I bought into the look, I'd want to destroy it. The feeling of being part of a pack never felt good. So I ended up with very confused looks – like the dullest Jaeger office-wear paired with a fur coat, flares and a dog collar.

I think the moment I really broke free was at my school graduation which was supposed to be black tie. It didn't seem fair to me that boys had to wear black and white while girls got to choose dresses in any colour they liked. So I bought a suit from a charity shop, superglued plastic dolls and fake flowers all over it, and then sprayed the whole thing with glitter. It was so coated in glue it didn't move when I walked. I remember the genuine anger directed at me for wearing it to a graduation, and found it really odd. It's just clothing, it's just some fabric. I definitely loved how much it upset people.

I think I enjoy tapping into different parts of my personality. I love dressing the way I do because it's freeing – clothes help me discover things about myself that I didn't know existed. I love to wear a suit as much as a fishnet catsuit, maybe like an actor trying on different characters depending on my mood.

George Bourgeois

I feel like I have two identities – on and off stage – and my style has split to reflect those two personalities. By day I don't have a major desire to be noticed anymore, whereas at night, on stage, I'm on full display. I think identity has a lot to do with it, as well as environment. I think what you wear can also impact your identity – clothes can let you become someone else, maybe someone you rarely show to the world.

In the right circumstances a strong look can give me confidence, can make me feel sexy and elegant and powerful. In the wrong circumstances it can make me feel very overdressed and like I wish I'd just worn jeans.

The map of the world waistcoat I'm wearing for my daywear photo means the most to me of any item of clothing I own. My mother gave it to me about 15 years ago; I think she found it in a charity shop. I've thrown or given away so many pieces over time but I can't get rid of this. When I first started going to clubs in London I wore it a lot – it actually led to a couple introducing themselves on a club dancefloor, and ten years later they are two of my closest friends and collaborators.

My hopes for the future? Personally, I hope I get to keep producing work and conquer the signs of my double chin. Globally, I hope the world calms the hell down."

George Bourgeois

Massimiliano Mocchia di Coggiola
Writer, illustrator, portrait painter, music video stylist & lecturer on fashion history

"I have the deep conviction to wear what appears to me as timeless and elegant. My desire to be atemporal makes me an eccentric in these times devoted to sanctification of well-being and appearance. However, I am not doing it to contrast with fashion: if tomorrow the trend becomes double-breasted suits, hard collars and ties, I wouldn't change my style.

The majority of my wardrobe comes from the Market of Vintage: I travel a lot, and that gives me the chance to discover many vintage shops that offer me the opportunity to expand my collection. On the side, I am passionate about custom-made clothes. I like to choose the fabrics, the cut and the details that make the suit unique and personal. All the clothes I buy systematically go through the tailor for alterations before entering my wardrobe.

In my teens, I was passionate about cinema (from the Twenties to Forties) where I found my inspirations. I was a boy who was different, shy, maybe too sensitive; my clothes gave me a kind of social justification to 'be strange'. I was about 14 when my parents took me to buy a new pair of shoes and I insisted on getting (without any difficulties) a pair of leather shoes instead of the umpteenth pair of sports shoes. This was the beginning of the end!

I feel this need to prove that appearance is as important as substance; even, that the outside expresses the best of what is inside, even if that point of view isn't shared or understood by everybody. Then there is my love for art, for colours and their combinations, that I am attempting to show through my look... and my interior decoration, my writing, my parties...

If I wasn't dressed the way I am, the people who I am interacting with wouldn't have the same level of interest toward me, my ideas and my work. I think that a part of my (small) success in my field is owed to my way of dressing.

My hopes for the future? To die like Sardanapale: beleaguered by the Barbarians, setting myself and my castle on fire, with my dogs, my horses, my wives and my servants."

Meihui Liu *Fashion designer, artist, curator & restaurateur*

"Be a creator, not a follower."

"I do think my identity defines what I wear.
But what does it say about me? Stubborn? Ghoulish? Angry? Foolish?
I'll take any of them.

I grew up in the first generation of what I call 'billboard culture': where the name/logo on your shirt, your trainers, your underwear, became all-important; if only because then everyone knew how much you'd paid for them. I remember a kid at my school who had trainers that cost £80. In 1985. I think they were luminous orange.

Idiotic. I had an immediate aversion to this, finding it to be just another symptom of Thatcherism and the hunt for the ultimate vacuity of the ultimate status symbol. The apogee of emptiness as the greatest ambition. This kind of artless-bullshit-thinking is with us still, in fact has become the overriding dogma of our times.

Turning goth at the age of 15, 16, had a lot to do with me going my own way in style, but then Bowie had a lot to do with that – Bowie meant that make-up was a definite option. The goth thing still hangs on in there with regards to my somewhat fractious relationship with colour; to this day I only ever wear red, black or grey. Oh, tell a lie, I have a green T-shirt. Never wear it, though."

Mason Ball / Benjamin Louche *Cabaret host & painted fool*

Tamer Wilde *Fashion stylist & director*

"I look back on photos from my childhood now and think, how oblivious was I not to notice how little I fit in? But it was honest oblivion. I just lived in my own world and knew nothing of what was considered convention at the time.

As far back as I can remember I pretty much always used to rummage through my grandmother's wardrobe and alter my own clothing. I got made fun of by my peers and told off by my teachers, but I guess I just had a warped reality. I grew up with no idea of pop culture since I had no television.

My father was a very eccentric and stylish man. He wore bespoke Savile Row suits and owned tons of Cuban heels in different colours and leathers. The black fur felt trilby he gave me means most to me of any items of clothing I own.

Dad's record collection was all either classical or disco, so I would just look at these beautiful artworks from artists like Sylvester, or the way they painted Bach and Tchaikovsky. At the time I was also obsessed with Oscar Wilde and the way he would describe the fashions of each of his characters.

So I guess these things greatly influenced my perspective on how to dress. But then I would mix it with leather biker jackets and torn jeans, so not quite sure where that came from.

I was always wearing things that reflected the way I felt. But never based on who I was or where I came from, because that is a huge melting pot that I wouldn't even know where to begin with.

I really don't limit myself on particular places to look for clothing, I have collected garments from all over the world, from

Tamer Wilde

handmade things by indigenous tribes to designers, to random thrift stores in middle America.

In all honesty I have never thought about the way I dress but more about what I like and what I dislike. I believe that style is something that is very personal to the individual. Fashion is what you wear; style is how you wear it. You can put the same jacket on 100 people and not one of them will look the same in it.

Some of my now personal friends tell me that upon introduction they assumed I didn't like them and that I was a little intimidating. But then on the flip side others have told me they immediately connected with me. On both ends of that spectrum they ended up becoming very close to me and seeing that there is a human being inside who is very real and very considerate, respectful and loyal.

I don't waste time criticising the way others look and think it's a huge sign of weakness when I see others do so. I will only take time to compliment people and sometimes it scares them.

As people we can hear a million compliments and only choose to respond to the negative comments someone makes, so I consciously do the opposite. Don't waste your time talking to someone that doesn't get you. Invest your energy on those who do. You'll live a better life.

I have never really had a Plan B. My whole life is based on the idea that if I'm not doing what I love right now then I am not alive."

Tamer Wilde

Eszter Karpati *Editor*

Magdalene Celeste *Costumier, fashion designer, model, professional glamourpuss, etc.*

"I love having my own likes and dislikes and I guess the way I dress is one expression of that. It all comes down to that complex and intangible construct of personal taste.

Discovering films like *Annie Hall* and *Jules et Jim* as a teenager definitely inspired me. My childhood friend always remembers with great affection the time when I drew on a thin moustache with my mother's eyeliner and announced that a drawn-on moustache was a great look for women – that must have been an influence of *Jules et Jim*.

One of my favourite people is Grayson Perry – I love the way he constantly challenges the way we perceive others, not just through his art but also the way he is. When he is dressed as Claire, his behaviour is still the same – the challenge is in the eyes of the beholder: can we relate to him the same way? That's the question."

"Dressing can be a great pleasure and I consider it an art form. The urge is creative; it's a compulsion to create in the same way as a painter or other type of artist. It is also a skill – style cannot be bought.

As long as I can remember I have had an obsession with beautiful clothing. I used to kick and scream when being 'persuaded' to wear jeans or sensible shoes as a child. I make most of my own clothes as I am dissatisfied with the quality of materials and the boring designs of mainstream fashion. I feel fully myself when wearing my own handmade clothing.

My mood defines what I choose to wear. Sometimes I wear a certain look because I want to get a particular response from others in a particular context. My clothes help me to balance myself out, so I will compensate for or underplay elements of my psyche according to how I feel. Mostly it's just showing off though."

Tuttii Fruittii *JüNgÒla DrâGKLòWN & technicolour hair sculptor*

"Take life with a pinch of salt; we are all human, we are all connected as one.
Let down your barriers, let down your negative views, and the life you lead
will be full of happiness and love."

"I was born in Rio de Janeiro, Brazil, in a revolutionary family. My parents are both social and political militants, hence non-conformism is in my DNA. I have a unique attitude and lifestyle: I don't follow trends, I live according to my own beliefs and individual tastes, and not according to society's standards. And that's expressed in the way I dress.

Yes, I'm a natural-born punk. Since my childhood I was always against the system and the established rules. I always used to have my eccentric preferences and do things differently from most people.

I wear my personality with originality. For me that's having style.

Unfortunately, in Brazil people still follow established conventions and are very judgemental about others who are outside the box, and when I moved to London I felt quite the opposite. I felt totally free there and it brought out all my fearlessness and creativity in dressing whatever way I wanted, not caring about what people would think of me. From then on I started to love being really daring in my style.

I'm very inspired by the whole Post-modernism movement, by Helmut Newton's work, and by my greatest muse, Grace Jones.

I still want to travel a lot around the world and go to a lot of new beautiful places, see different cultures and meet interesting people. I am very curious and excited about new things and new experiences. I want to continuously expand as much as I can.

I love to provoke. I want to touch and move others. Admiration, strangeness, curiosity, inspiration... mixed feelings. As long as they feel something."

Jana Mello *Fashion stylist & costume designer*

James Theseus Buck *Artist*

"I've always wanted to be a wizard,
  and in some ways that has never changed."

"When I wore panda make-up to BoomBox (a weekly themed party that attracts many creative individuals), the following month my photo was in *Vogue*, *Elle*, *Dazed & Confused*, *Pop*, leading to lots of interview requests. It was the moment I moved away from being a fashion-lover to a visual storyteller and performance artist.

As a performance artist I am very aware there is a true self and there is a presented public 'self'. When I don't work I am a mum, so I am relaxed, comfortable, focused and functional. As an artist I choose my appearance and clothing carefully depending on what I am representing: sometimes I am strong and powerful, sometimes I am fragile and vulnerable. I use make-up, costume, installation to help me communicate my ideas with the audiences. Their reactions and interactions help complete my performance as a whole."

Echo Morgan *Illustrator & performance artist*

"I think identity and style definitely go hand in hand; what you choose to wear may represent your personality, however it certainly does not say everything.

When I pop to the shops for groceries, I tend to go 'in disguise' – *a.k.a.* in your average joggers and hoodie – and keep myself to myself, whereas, of course, if I am looking my best I 'perform' better socially. If I go out in drag for example, which I sometimes do, then a strange surge of energy and confidence is there. As if you are almost playing a character. You can challenge people a bit more and have a lot of fun with it.

I don't buy many clothes any more; I have a bunch of key pieces I repeat. My mum passed down a Vivienne Westwood velvet jacket with a huge fluffy collar and cuffs. I also could never part with my custom-made leather jacket by Nympha; on the back, it has me eating a banana and winking plus 'BANKS' printed too. Very narcissistic!"

Louie Banks *Fashion & celebrity photographer*

Yusura *Aerial fire-based circus performer, actor & model*

"Everything comes from my spirit.
 There is no why, it's just natural for me to dress the way I do."

Le Gateau Chocolat *Performer & opera singer*

"Were there signs of non-conforming from an early age? If a young, Nigerian boy – four, maybe – wearing his sister's bathing suit at a local swimming pool counts, then yup.

I dress the way I do for my sense of self. Sometimes out of defiance, when I have the energy to wage war against conformity or stereotype, but mostly it's merely how I feel and who I am.

Clothes have always been a means of self-expression. Being Rubenesque always meant having to go bespoke or searching for one-offs as I could never fit into the homogenous/mass-produced which was both incredibly frustrating and fortuitous.

I get my clothes everywhere. I don't discriminate. If it calls, I answer.

I don't care what people think when they see me – or I'd really like not to. Honestly, I'd like to be able to turn off the side of me that cares. Part of me still does because they stare, gawp, point, take pictures, murmur, etc., and the rest of me is tired of caring.

In future, I plan to excavate further into being me. Fearlessly so. This is it; no second chances, just now. Go for it. Unashamedly."

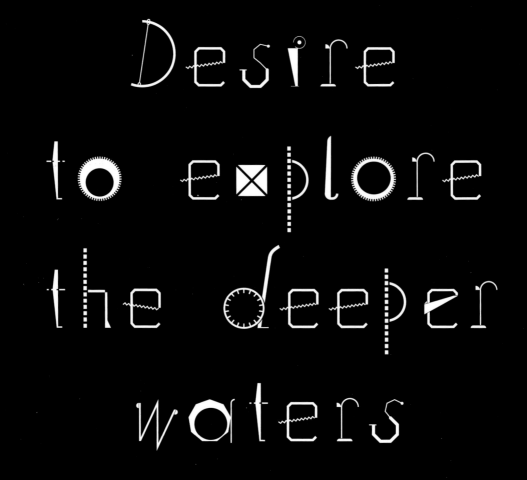

Desire to explore the deeper waters

Erika Dark *Fashion designer*

"I'm an introverted extrovert. Days when I dress 'loudest' are the ones when I want to hide from everyone the most. It makes people feel too intimidated to approach me."

Tony Sylvester *Musician, writer & umbrella salesman*

"There's a Japanese expression *kata* which is the idea that there are a certain amount of rules that come with any skills you learn as a profession; the idea that an apprentice learns everything meticulously and only at that point can they break away. I think that's very, very important. Aged 42, I think I'm only just at the level of self-confidence and knowledge about the history of clothes and style, that I really feel I can.

I still work very much within the parameters of the last 100 years and the way men have dressed. I know there are other people in this book who are about questioning gender and all sorts of conventions, but I'm really trying to find some level of comfort, some kind of confidence in myself.

I wear vintage, bespoke and a lot of more modern things too. I'm interested in the way that clothes from different eras work together, rather than the differences. The only conventions I have broken free of are the shackles of the modern day.

Growing up, I was really into skateboarding which led into hardcore and punk. How I wanted to dress came from what I saw on record covers or American magazine covers. But thirty years ago, you couldn't buy a pair of Vans in England other than via mail order from a skate shop outlet. I saved up for my first pair, second-hand, which were 30 quid, an astronomical amount at the time. Now everyone from toddlers through to cool dads wear Vans. A lot of these things – Champion hooded sweatshirts, flannel shirts, really dark Levi's 501s – as a teenager, I fetishised from afar but just couldn't get.

A big moment was definitely getting my hands tattooed. Nowadays, kids do the extremities then fill in, but the hand tattoos were the final step for me, and I didn't get them until my early thirties. After that I started dressing more conservatively, covering up the rest of them. Some notion of smartening up came along with those hand tattoos.

In 2009, Scott Schuman, founder of *The Sartorialist*, shot me for Burberry, in a Mark Powell [see page 62] flannel suit and holding a pocket watch, and the image

Tony Sylvester

really struck a chord. At that point, I don't think many people had seen someone dressing quite smart, very tailored, but with a beard and heavily tattooed.

I grew a beard at 21, and I'd get shouted at in the street, called a 'tramp'. You did not see young people with beards twenty years ago. Now beards have become mainstream. I think that's where being older, and having seen these cycles of fashion, puts you in better stead, because you realise that for most people these things are fleeting. I have a beard because I look better with a beard.

People comment to me on the contradiction that I was this guy who grew up in hardcore, is heavily tattooed, and looks, perhaps, a bit scary, but at the same time I try to present myself in a slightly more rarefied, sophisticated way. That sits strangely with people, and I like the fact it does. I get a kick out of people being a little bit bemused; that's the pay-off.

The item of clothing I have the most emotional attachment to is a bespoke pair of tartan trews in the Campbell tartan – the family tartan of my late mum – which I had made for my wedding by Fred Nieddu, an incredible cutter with an amazing eye for detail and similar taste to me. We both like really high waists: basically, below the nipple… well, definitely on the ribs – a gentleman dresses from his shoulders, not from the waist!

The way trews are made, there is no seam, so it's one piece of tartan, with a pocket cut into the sides. They took three or four hours to press, just manipulating the wool, the fabric to get a line on them. A hell of a lot of work went into them so I'm very appreciative of them and I wear them still.

What a tragedy it would be to drop down dead before getting my money's worth from such clothes. It's all very well having clothes that will outlive me, but, by God, let's hope I get the chance to put some wear into them."

Tony Sylvester

Angel Rose *Artist*

Valeria Agostini *Milliner, artist & performer*

"I like to use my appearance to surprise people, to subvert their expectations by playing with certain contrasts.

Obviously I am quite invested in goth and punk subcultures, but people are often surprised when they meet me to discover that my look is much darker than my attitude! In part I owe this to my stylistic icon, Elvira, who embodied both the undead vamp as well as the ditzy California valley girl.

My artistic heroines are people such as Orlan, Kembra Pfahler and Lydia Lunch, all of whom, in their own way, push their femininity to extremes. I like juxtapositions they inhabit – a mix between the glamorous and the gruesome, the feminine and the fearsome.

My favourite quotation? 'Tonight is the future' – Tony Manero in *Saturday Night Fever*."

"I was born in Norrköping, Sweden, but as a teenager growing up in Bavaria I used to go to a lot of medieval parties in castle ruins and outdoor gothic festivals and dressed like a medieval gothic *Burgfräulein*: very heavily made up, complete with hennin – a pointed headdress and long veiling that I made myself. We'd read poetry and listen to gothic/medieval music all night long.

The clothes that mean most to me are a vintage dirndl (traditional dress in Austria and Bavaria) from my mum, and a studded Versace leather jacket, because it's just perfect.

My hope for the future? To make a hat for the Queen."

Coco Fennell *Womenswear designer*

"I've always dressed silly – my whole family does. I think it's in my blood.
I just like shiny over-the-top things!"

"Since I was a toddler I have been obsessed with female icons, especially female villain characters. My first inspiration was The Wicked Queen from *Snow White*, who I used to dress up as when I was two years old – my mother even made me a cape like hers. I would play for hours in the back garden, re-enacting scenes from the film.

After The Wicked Queen I quickly moved onto The Wicked Witch of The West, Ursula from *The Little Mermaid*, and then came Elvira, Bette Midler (Winifred Sanderson in *Hocus Pocus*), Bernadette Peters (as the Witch in *Into the Woods*) and so many more. Virgin is informed by all of these characters and many of these references are visible in her look.

Style and dress are an expression of something felt deep within the wearer of the outfit; it's an outward comment of something internal, and personal. As Andrew, I dress quite boringly because I've never really been interested in men's fashion, and so I don't invest much in my own look as a boy.

When I am dressed as Virgin, I act entirely differently. I hold myself differently, I speak in her accent, even when I'm not on stage – I can't help it! There's three hours of make-up, six-inch heels, huge headpieces, and long sparkling gowns and veils standing in the way between Andrew and Virgin, so when she's 'on', she's on. She takes over.

My own identity is present in Virgin due to my Catholic upbringing, and also going to Catholic school as a gay boy who was usually made fun of for being 'weird' or 'different'. I found the character of the Virgin Mary comforting; I remember being in church looking at her statue with that vacant, sombre look on her face and thinking: 'I bet you actually look nothing like that. I bet you're actually completely fabulous, colourful, and full of energy and resilience because of all the shit you've been through.'

I always thought of the Virgin Mary as a strong, confident, opinionated woman, a total eccentric, who was probably completely insane because of her traumatic past – nothing like the way she was ever portrayed in the church. But I now get to portray her the way I envisage her, as Virgin Xtravaganzah."

Andrew Burt a.k.a. Virgin Xtravaganzah *Performer*

David Wood *Co-founder & art director of a fetish/body art club, etc.*

"I loved military uniforms from a very young age. My brother was in the army and I used to love to try all his hats on. When we played war games at school from the age of six I always wanted to be a Nazi or Japanese soldier because they had better uniforms and were more exotic and I loved doing the opposite of what everyone else wanted to do.

Also as a young child I loved the theatricality of silent horror films with Lon Chaney or German Expressionism, and the cartoon TV show *Mr Ben*. My first sexual fantasies were about these women in shiny silver sci-fi outfits in a TV show called *UFO*. So most of my visual obsessions and fantasies were all there from a very young age.

As a teenager I was into the skinhead/2tone scenes before switching to new romantic/ goth/industrial, and I've always liked looks that contrast half-violent thug with camp dandy. Later, I was wearing fetish clothing in the early 1980s even before I knew what fetish was. As soon as I saw it I knew it was for me.

At the peak of being a goth in the early Eighties at art school I wouldn't go and buy a pint of milk from the corner shop without spending three or four hours to do my hair, make-up and dressing up. The look was 24/7.

Dressing in full fetish wear in the day time, with a face full of theatrical make-up, big hair, nose chain and dog skull on my crotch, etc. – I used to love to shock and provoke people as much as possible. And I got bottled by a gang of mods, chased by skinheads, head-butted, nose chain ripped through my nose, threatened with a knife, finger broken, and very narrowly escaped being killed by a gang. That was normal then and in a way I loved it. Especially when walking past a gang that wanted to kill me for looking gay with the best-looking girl they'd ever seen on my arm giving them loads of attitude. Every day you would literally fight for your self-expression.

David Wood

I don't care what people in the street think of me now. Now in the day-time I just want to function, get on with life and get from A to B, ideally in a taxi. It became liberating to not always care that much. There's work time, relaxing time, dressing-up time, fantasy time.

If you fully explore yourself, what you are truly into and your fantasies, then the way you look should reflect that. Dressing up is a way of being honest with who you are but it can also be a fun way of self-expression, and sometimes dressing up as a completely different character can be even more fun. Why just be one character forever when you can be multiple characters and go on a journey?"

David Wood

Eloise Chong-Gargette *Archivist*

Nikita Andrianova *Brand development & styling creative*

"Early signs of non-conforming? I made up dance moves to *Starman* when I was six. Does that count?"

"At the age of 18, I wanted to be noticed, I wanted to have fun. I was all about colour, mix-and-match and madness. Later on, I found more pleasure in a more minimal style. Now I keep my palette black; the only exceptions I make are a bit of burgundy on rare occasions and some naturals – nude shades, dark browns, greys and white.

I prefer to focus on the details in jewellery, make-up and accessories and add a bit of colour and twist to the look that way. I like giving classics an edge and adding kinky details to simple looks. The urge is to be creative about every part of my life."

James Edward Quaintance *Model/actor*

"I'm a 'slashy' – LOL – a model/actor, and not the other way round.
I was the middle child, always out of the house, doing his own thing –
you know, 'the rebel'. Growing up in Venice, California, I would skate
in suits and was always doing my own thing style-wise too… still am."

Mara de Nudée *Burlesque dancer, singer & actress*

Laura Cogoni *Ceramic artist & healer*

Ian Bruce *Musician*

Mickael Francois Loir *Founder & director of male accessories brand, etc.*

▸

"My great-grandmother's black day dress, my grandmother's shirts, my mother's christening dress made by her grandmother… surprisingly, these are not the clothes I wear, but they mean the world to me."

◢

Mara de Nudée

▸

"I prefer to be naked most of the time. When I'm not naked I wear black with quartz crystal jewellery. I like to feel like an FBI agent on a catwalk.

From an early age, I never gave a shit about being in anyone's group or being friends with any one particular person. I wanted all and everyone.

The turning point with regard to my style came when I was at a club in Coventry and every girl had the same-length, straightened, blonde hair and one of these girls asked me why I dressed like a weirdo. Because I had long black hair in a topknot and I wasn't wearing the standard mini-skirt with my tits out.

The urge to dress the way I do comes from not having an urge – it comes from being myself, being free, being able to think in a non-linear way and be imaginative with my footsteps."

◢

Laura Cogoni

"There were definitely signs of me being a relatively obnoxious show-off from a young age! 'Look at me, Mum.'

I can't imagine going on stage without wearing full costume. Like donning armour for battle. It makes me feel invincible in front of a crowd and gives me the power to show off to the best of my abilities.

It's a simple formula: looking different makes you feel different, makes you act different. The costumes are functional as much as aesthetic; it doesn't feel inappropriate to sweat into them profusely.

I want to keep spinning all the plates: singing, painting, animation, dildo design and whatever else tickles my fancy. But most importantly I want to balance this with time spent with my girlfriend and friends."

Ian Bruce

"Our days are constrained and the temptations of mediocrity are plentiful. Remaining elegant is for me a constant challenge that I take up daily. I wish to keep on breaking the monotony and triviality of the everyday."

Mickael Francois Loir

Anett-Patrice Van York *Art director & photographer*

"I was born in Germany, and I grew up in the North near Hamburg near the sea. When I was eighteen-and-a-half I moved to Paris to study fashion design at the great Haute Couture school Chambre Syndicale de la Couture Parisienne, one of the best fashion schools in the world. I stayed in Paris for six years, and worked for great couture houses like Christian Dior, Balmain and Mugler.

I always liked the avant-garde, the most important items of clothing are my original Lee Alexander McQueen gowns (when he was still alive) because he was my favourite fashion designer of the last decade; the decade before it was Thierry Mugler for me.

I get my clothes from the design headquarters, or from sample sales, or from design outlets, all over the world. Also, I like to mix and match expensive clothes with second-hand clothes sometimes. I love Paris's second-hand stores and markets or London's Camden Town markets.

The first turning point of my life was when I moved to Paris and studied at this extraordinary Haute Couture school. I was in my element and surrounded by people with the same ideas and the same creative gifts. I am a very visual and very creative person. The second was when I moved from Paris to New York, where I stayed for 14 years, I continued my studies there in fashion marketing. In New York I could express my style and creativity even more, because the scene in New York was, and still is, much more extreme than it ever was in Paris.

I was always very different than my conservative family. They never really understood me, so I created my own family around me with my best friends who are like me, especially my very long-time and best friends in New York, who have known me and loved me for over 20 years now.

Yes, my identity defines what I choose to wear: I am an avant-garde person, I like everything that is not conformist, and of course I choose McQueen, because he was the best. Nobody like McQueen. I miss him terribly.

Anett-Patrice Van York

When people see me in the streets, I would like them to think I am a cool person, not a boring, conservative one. And that it is only the surface; people should look deeper and should be more spiritual and more psychologically trained nowadays. I don't want to be judged by my outside, but by my inside. I have a very good heart, and I am the best friend that you can have.

The way I dress comes naturally, because it's fun and I am in my element when I do it. It is like breaking out and being free again, I get bored tremendously with conservative people. And when you dress up you meet fast, like-minded people, especially in London and New York.

The way I present myself doesn't affect my behaviour; I am the way I am. I only feel more comfortable, more like myself when I can dress up, and it's easier to meet like-minded people like that too.

I have lived all over the world, I am a very open-minded and cool person, and it's fun to dress up but a human being is more than that. And people should know I am an Aquarius. You never get bored with Aquarians. Aquarians need to feel free and have fun!

My favourite quote? 'I am my own rule!'"

Anett-Patrice Van York

Camilla Yadgaroff *Design studio manager*

"I've worn black every day for the last ten years as I have a great affinity with the dark side. Although as my style started to develop, I wanted to make sure that my femininity was an equal focus."

Daniel Lismore *Artist*

"I'm a full-time artist; I live as art.

Sometimes I indulge in the creative process of making couture or creating visuals for celebrities, fashion and make-up brands. I also make perfume.

In 2016, an exhibition of my clothing started touring the world – 3,800 pieces that have been assembled into 32 life-size sculptures of myself. Putting that together brought so many memories back. Like walking to the shops in the village where I was raised wearing make-up, an orange ripped-up tie-dye top, a pair of giant Swear platforms that resembled moon boots, flared jeans ripped up to my crotch, make-up, braided hair and a hippie necklace. I was only 15. A car stopped and another beeped and nearly crashed.

Growing up, I liked dressing how I felt was fun. Then I spent some time with the Masai. There I understood what it was like to be a human without material things. I watched the tribes of Kenya dress and I learned a lot from them with their draping and jewellery embellishment.

I now find my clothing on my travels around the globe – from mountain villages to couture ateliers in Paris, charity shops and the streets of London, the Masai Mara to young British designers. I just throw things on and in the mix. I like thinking of myself as a canvas and only look at colour, shape and texture.

Of course I conform from time to time; it's part of being human. But I've always tried to escape those thoughts. I have done my best to be myself, and maybe that's what a lot of the population may lack at times, but I have to conform to not to fit in.

We need to sort out the global-warming crisis or soon everyone will be wearing clothes like me because there will be mass destruction and people will have to go back to basics, wearing ripped fabrics draped over their shoulders.

When people see me, I don't want them to think. I want people to walk past and acknowledge that it is normal. Which sometimes happens, but only in London.

Daniel Lismore

I attract the extremes in society and in culture. Obsession, love... intrigued people or those who want to kill me, hurt me and put me down. Usually I'm well armed with jewellery and chainmail so I embrace all situations."

Daniel Lismore

Veroni Deco *Creative soul & fashion designer*

"Clothing and shoes are important accessories with which to dress up your body and mind. I believe suitable clothing gives your mind a lift, boosts confidence and underlines your personality so that you can become a flower to curious bees."

"I was born with bells on (literally). It was early morning in 1965 via an army ambulance with motorcycle escort across the wet country roads of Suffolk. My finale was a caesarean at Colchester's Military Hospital. My mother died (briefly) but was coaxed back by a Victorian 'ghost' clad in high collar and topper, wearing a watch chain. Medical staff based at the 19th-century institution (now demolished) acknowledged numerous sightings of the benevolent spectre.

I have reacted towards and against many things in my life – all contribute to who I am now and how I portray myself aesthetically. For me, being in a desired atmosphere is of paramount importance (or it's rope-dangle time). As far back as I can remember I created a bubble to survive in, surrounded by what I'd consider to be beautiful *objet d'horreur*. My nights are enhanced by a swirling psychedelic liquid light projection wheel, Sixties Hammond organ and sitar and I have a zero-tolerance policy on all gel-haired, pip-squeak TV presenters and advertisements (hence I've not had a television in years).

I live in a Regency townhouse with an ornate balcony overlooking a bruised Brighton ocean and live perpetually in my early-Seventies British Amicus horror fantasy and dress accordingly. This suits me dandily. Should I venture out I merely divert my gaze from pedestrian ugliness. I mean where's our individuality and sartorial inheritance now? We live in a weeping fissure of energy-saving bulbs; sent to bed early by our financial controllers. The sound of spanking pert bottoms under hitched-up lace and velvets has been usurped by the sound of idiots applauding their false Emperor's panda 'onesie'. Decades of British elegance have been strangled by multinational corporations cloaked beneath a guise of convenience, comfort and conformity.

My hope for the future is that, collectively, we actually learn to think for ourselves, develop the balls to openly question the unquestionable and take back the knowledge that belongs to us all. If that sounds paranoid then all I can say is do your own research."

Atters Attree *Interdimensional out-of-body explorer*

Pandemonia Panacea *Fine artist*

"The urge to dress the way I do comes from a wish to affect and comment on the world. Through the power of image I can harness social media to spread my work and ideas. I wear my identity like a piece of clothing. My face is my logo – instantly recognisable; hair – my trademark; dress – emblem of femininity.

In the mid-2000s, exasperated by the tabloid press and celebrity culture, I designed and created my own celebrity to feed back to the media their own values. I've just taken part in an advert for Camper. My image right now is being daubed on the walls of Paris. It is a fantastic piece of *detournement*.

The way I present myself allows me to go to places you can't normally go to, and talk to people you can't normally talk to. When people see me I'd like them to think about their own sense of agency and, of course, take a photo and spread the message.

In my case, my identity doesn't define what I choose to wear. Quite the opposite. What I wear defines my identity, just like the Trojan Horse."

Mark Charade *DJ & videographer*

"The item that means most to me is one of the simplest I have: a plain black wool suit. I wore it for my grandfather's funeral. My grandparents played a big role in raising me, so I suppose I had a somewhat old-fashioned upbringing and was taught to be quite the gentleman. Some of it stuck, I guess.

I'm very slim. I wear a 32-inch chest so my options are, sadly, somewhat limited. Some of my clothes come from the occasional trawl through the few retailers that stock my sizes. I'm usually out of luck, but every now and then I'll find one or two rare gems that I see potential in. Some stuff is even from Korea due to their smaller sizes. Combining items with a well-chosen pocket square, pin or chain, etc. is a really simple way to elevate an otherwise simple outfit and add a personal flair to it. For these I'll typically hunt through vintage stores, ebay and Etsy and combine elements.

I was never one for machismo. The combination of me being so slim, and the blandness of the vast majority of men's clothing available led me to take a DIY approach with unisex clothes, or rather, clothes cut for girls. This afforded me a certain level of peacocking and androgyny inspired by the likes of David Bowie, Marc Bolan and Bauhaus.

My father's vinyl collection was also an endless mine of inspiration. Sometimes I'd sneak into it just to look at all the amazing artwork. When most kids my age were listening to Take That or Ace of Base, I was listening to Frank Zappa and Captain Beefheart. There was never really going to be much hope for me.

As a kid, just before discovering the post-punk bands that would have a more meaningful effect on me, I remember reading about The Sex Pistols and being inspired by the bold, DIY attitude of the movement. I chopped up an old shirt and jacket and drew designs on them. I even adorned an old suitcase with images cut out from *Tank Girl* comics. That was the first time I customised and created my own outfit and wore it out of the house. Oh how I would cringe if I could see it now!

In all honesty, my outfits are often louder than I am in public. I'm incredibly passionate

Mark Charade

about the people I love, the things that inspire me, and my creative work but you won't find me in a club jumping up on the tables and pelvic-thrusting. I'm not that guy.

I suppose another element of my identity is my approach to gender. (Not just in terms of appearance, but everyday attitudes and roles.)

However easy, neat and simple it is to think in binary terms, I consider gender to be like jazz. You can play your own tune, improvise and experiment and, through that freedom of expression, gender identity can evolve and change over time. From Bowie and Prince to Marlene Dietrich, I've always found artists that subvert gender norms incredibly interesting.

I used to dress far more androgynously. Lately, with the moustache and suits in addition to the make-up, it's kind of come full circle where it's almost a kind of exaggerated vaudevillian parody of an old-fashioned dandy.

My style comes from a desire to pay homage to my inspirations and explore or exaggerate facets of my personality. It's a way of wearing my heart on my sleeve.

I'm also lucky enough that my girlfriend of many years is also a well-dressed aesthete who appreciates a good suit like many gentlemen appreciate lingerie. I suppose, when we go out together, I see putting care into my appearance as not only an act of self-respect, but also respect for her. I don't take her for granted so I'm always trying to woo her.

I dress for myself and my partner. If I'm DJing at an event then my dress is intended to heighten the aesthetic experience. On the street I'm far less concerned with people's opinions. The simple combination of facial hair and make-up is too much for many people, so asking them to think about much at all is perhaps an exercise in futility."

Mark Charade

"I was always allowed to choose what I wanted to wear. My stepmother said to me: 'Robin, you have something special – don't ever let anyone take that from you.' It meant it was okay to express myself and be who I was from a very young age. That has made me what I am today.

Interesting story: I dressed as a poodle for a Halloween party about ten years ago and just woofed at everyone the whole night. So much fun. About three weeks later I was walking down Brick Lane in London, not wearing the poodle outfit, and a passing group of Italians put there paws up and said, 'Woof woof' to me! Having fun is so simple."

Robin Pawloski *Hair stylist*

"I grew up in Russia where standing out is not a good thing. Everyone was beige and grey; I wanted variety and magic. I wanted to try on different masks, imagine myself as different people and characters and tell stories by dressing up.

My Orthodox priestess headdress probably means most to me of all the clothing items I own as it was one of the first theatrical pieces that I designed and commissioned, and a symbol that constantly reappears in my work."

Karina Akopyan *Artist & illustrator*

"I try not to spend my life worrying about what other people think of me. I remember a moment as a young teenager at the seaside with my family. My granny was holding up a towel for me to change into my swimming costume behind. Accidentally she lost her grip and dropped the towel, revealing a naked me. I was furious but my granny pointed out calmly and clearly that no one on the beach was looking at me or, indeed, interested. One of many wonderful life lessons from my granny."

Nisha: "As I've got older I've become more interested in expressing my heritage through my clothing, and often incorporate Indian clothes and jewellery into my outfits. When Amber and I are together people constantly ask if we're twins. Or if we're wearing wigs!"

Amber: "I take quite a character-based approach to getting dressed – anyone from Carmen Miranda to the art teacher in *Ghost World* – so I'm not sure what that says about my own identity! Sometimes people in the street tell me I've cheered them up because of all the colour. Which always makes me happy."

Rachel May Snider *Performer, maker & writer*

Amber *Fashion historian* & Nisha *Interior designer, a.k.a.* Broken Hearts *DJs*

Carley Hague *Tailor, stylist & performer*

"I dress like I draw or paint. My body is a canvas and I hang trinkets and jewels upon it that highlight and adorn it with beauty and grace, intrigue, explosions of colour and patterns. I guess you could say this is how my brain works. I've experienced the other worlds, and I want to express their beauty in my dress and home.

Comically, my good friend suggested that my eye for the unusual was purely down to the fact that I was a one-way tripper never coming back – thanks, Carrie! In that case, I must have been tripping since I was born.

Day to day, I get mixed reactions, but I am mainly dressing to please myself more than others, so I don't really care. When I'm dressing to perform it gives me so much freedom to go to extreme levels; I can turn into whatever creature I so wish.

My favourite was a Halloween gig where I danced to The Prodigy's *Voodoo People* wearing full voodoo dress with white irises, ripping apart a cooked chicken I got from Tesco, spitting it all over the place, and also managing to spit fake blood on a pretty girl's fresh white ironed silk shirt – yes, she was disgusted, but, yes, I was delighted.

As a tailor, I want to make epic, beautiful pieces that start as garments and turn into pieces of art – it might take six months, but it will happen and they will be works of extreme beauty and craftsmanship. And I hope to just live a wonderful love-filled life as I do now. May the world and all its inhabitants find the divine light that lies within to lift all of our futures.

What I would like people to think, and what they do think about me when I walk down the street are two different things, but it would be nice if they were all like half the population, and thought: 'Ooh, she's brought a lot of colour and joy to this grey, boring street.'"

Lily Dean *Sculptor*

"When I was 12, I started listening to Marilyn Manson.
He taught me it was okay to be weird."

"As Grace Jones said:
'One creates oneself.'"

"My favourite quotation is from Anaïs Nin:
'Had I not created my own world, I would
certainly have died in other people's.'"

Amechi Ihenacho *Fashion designer, tailor, vintage shop & cocktail bar owner*

Hannah Bhuiya *Stylist*

Vicky Butterfly *Burlesque performance artist, costume-maker & show creator*

"I don't really remember a point where I haven't dressed differently. As a child I know my parents had unusual tastes but as soon as I was allowed to dress myself it never occurred to me that I shouldn't wear exactly what I wanted. And I have always admired others who did likewise, like the Marchesa Luisa Casati. I just wish I had her budget.

I don't think I ever really knew what conformity was. I knew that everything about my life was a bit different to my friends' but I think I realised at an early age that when I tried to fit in I never got it quite right.

Oscar Wilde said: 'One should either be a work of art, or wear a work of art.' I don't identify as much with the rest of the quotation, but it was the motto of a club I used to go to with religious fervour as a teenager where we all dressed exactly as we felt like.

I am very independent – I think I have always just gone my own way. I don't try and fit any particular era even though I love antique clothes. For me it is a lot about how it makes me feel: different patterns, textures and weights of fabric.

I rarely buy clothes anymore: I have a huge amount of vintage and make a lot myself. If I want something specific, ebay is helpful but generally I like to browse flea markets or buy friends' designs.

I wear the kind of things I like to look at. Why just look at something in a case or a picture when you can have it with you all the time?

The jewelled Victorian opera crowns and brassieres that I collect used to be the clothes I treasured most, but now it's a cap of my dad's. It's one of the only things I have of his: the rest of his clothes have been donated to the camps at Calais and it both reminds me of him and makes me hope for a brighter future for them."

Sue Kreitzman *Artist & writer*

> "I wear what I am compelled to wear, I wear my obsessions. I am a walking art gallery, a perambulating collage. I am an artist and collector; I wear my art and my collections with great pride.

I design my clothes and then have them stitched up by a local tailor. Or I collaborate with artists I love and mentor. All the fabrics I use in my own designs are collected by me in my travels. I haunt flea markets, bazaars, charity shops and ethnic markets.

Sometimes Diane Goldie reproduces my own paintings onto colourful kimonos of her design or my design, Anne-Sophie Cochevelou [see page 16] makes me a fabulous garment or piece of jewellery every few months – I just let her imagination run wild. Anothai Hansen and I collaborate on massive and fascinating necklaces. The necklaces I make myself are exuberant collections of found objects.

I have been avoiding 'fashion' and conventional style since I was a teenager, and I am now in my mid-seventies. In the Fifties when I was in high school, I hated the cashmere twin-sets (owned in every colour) that the girls wore, the pencil skirts, the gold circle pins, the tasteful strings of pearls, the gold charm bracelets, the poufy, swishy full skirts worn over horsehair crinolines, the penny loafers, the ballet flats... I hated

Sue Kreitzman

all of it, and never wore any of it. Everyone looked the same; it was incredibly boring and soul-destroying.

My parents had little money; my rich aunts used to send boxes of hand-me-downs for me to wear, and I had some really magnificent clothes from them, completely unlike anything the girls wore day to day in high school. I looked quite unlike everyone else. When I had some spare money (saved from babysitting and giving music lessons) I bought 'bohemian' copper jewellery in Greenwich Village in New York, and ethnic jewellery as well, and adorned my hand-me-downs with these lovely and fascinating pieces. I still have many of them today.

I am always dressed as exactly the person I really am. My outer trappings match my inner persona. It gives me supreme confidence because I am who I am, no disguise, no pretence, no trying to hide my inner self. It is all out there for everyone to see, and I am proud. People stop to talk, they take my picture, they smile as I walk by. I ignore those who shudder and look away!

I want people who see me on the street to be dazzled by the colour and the art. I want them to think: 'I want to do that!' I want them to go home and embrace colour and start making art. I want to change their lives. I also want them to realise that being old does not mean being moribund, boring, over the hill and on the scrap heap. But please realise: I am not really an old lady, just cleverly disguised as one."

Sue Kreitzman

Viktoria Modesta *Bionic pop artist*

"I think my favourite thing is when I've put a lot of thought into my outfit, but
it is quite subtle, elegant. It looks like I am not trying really hard, but once
someone pays attention, they notice exactly what is going on."

Charm

&

karma

Aymeric Bergada du Cadet *Stylist & artistic director*

"The lack of humanity in fashion pushed me to create my own vision.
 I don't like that in fashion you see the design before you see the human."

David Piper *Absurdist & global gin brand ambassador*

Bambi Blue *Showgirl & events organiser*

"Sometimes I just want to be a superhero. It can certainly be easier to be around other people if you inhabit a character who isn't entirely yourself (although very close… confusingly hard to tell apart, in fact), and clothes are perhaps the most obvious prop for that. But I've learnt to let a lot of that go.

My job now requires me to be 'on show' a little, in varied situations – but I feel it is important, better for everyone around, if that comes naturally, without trying to push too hard on first impression. So, if anything, I've toned down how I dress – I still want to have fun with it, but I'm cautious of getting lost in it.

Often I feel I'd rather be the same person, in unremarkable clothes, first, before adding layers of fun and fantasy on top."

"Around the second year I spent working as a full-time performer, my style shifted from a little quirky to full-on fruitcake, which I embraced entirely. I went through a break-up with someone who wasn't very supportive of my strangeness and that encouraged me to think 'who cares?'. Since letting go of conformity I have become much more bohemian in my mentality.

I think I just want to be a gypsy princess through and through. I like people guessing I'm a performer by my style and I like keeping elements of my showgirl attire in my everyday wear, like my signature flower pom-poms. I wear clamshell bras out a lot and like to explain to strangers that I'm a mermaid (I was born at the bottom of the sea out of a giant clamshell – from a mother of pearl called Jayne).

It's all about making the grey parts of town more colourful for me and expressing the freedom I feel inside to everyone else."

"I describe myself as a revolutionary activist because my desired changes go significantly beyond mere reform. I hope for a better tomorrow for us all: a world characterised by equality without conformity, a world of peace with justice (after Mandela's example of reconciliation), with a revived ethos that respects the limitations of our world, and all with a sense of humour – think a global Portmeirion, but with free folk not prisoners."

"People express themselves in all manner of ways. I think dressing practically is great too; it doesn't have to be flamboyant and avant-garde all the time. I don't think people should judge a person simply by their appearance and they should be free to express themselves however they want without prejudice. So if people want to judge that's up to them but I don't really care what people may conclude about me from a first glance."

Farhan Rasheed *Revolutionary activist*

Joe Miller *Designer vintage clothing business co-owner*

Soki Mak *Creative, art director & fashion stylist*

"My identity is much more than what I wear: my identity is my mind, my beliefs…
and maybe also my hair!"

"You gotta fight for
your right to be arty.
I like to bring back
fantasy and magic to
our world. I'm just one
of the characters of
a magical realm from
somewhere else that
is visiting our world.
I just like to be myself.
I interact with people in
the same way always; it
doesn't matter what I am
wearing. Just be free.

I believe your style is just an extension of your own self and your universe, what you want to share with the world. But obviously your style has to complement your true identity.

I don't really think about what other people think about me; you cannot be free if you do. But, in general, I get loads of smiles which is always nice. I get some compliments, some weird faces sometimes… and also quite a lot of people taking photos. Ha-ha."

Maria Almena *Multidisciplinary artist & creative director*

Alis Pelleschi *Visual artist & latex fashion brand co-director*

"My motto is: 'One day we're going to die, so why waste it worrying?' At one time, I was dealing with a lot of my own insecurities; anxiety and depression was an ever-present demon in my life. So I was trying to come up with a mantra to let go of these negative thoughts or anxieties. This made sense to me. I could spend the rest of my life worrying and being suppressed by it, to then die and it not mean anything anyway. Or I could just live my life, enjoy it and stop worrying.

I like to get dressed up every day even if I'm not going anywhere. When I'm dressed down or in 'conventional' ways I feel less confident, less myself. I walk stronger, I smile more when dressed as boldly as I feel that day.

I'm fascinated by how appearance/clothing can help define your own identity. I can leave the house without make-up on… except for pink lipstick (a habit I inherited from my mum). I can't go out without that.

In the last five years I've become more confident in who I am and what I'm about and my style goes along with that. But I still feel like I'm figuring it out. I like the idea that I can constantly evolve and change; it's why I love senior-style fashion so much. I hope by the age of 70 I will have figured it all out.

I was definitely a brave tester of fashion in my teens, and was regularly told, 'You can't go out dressed like that.' Growing up in the MySpace era, I loved dressing up and testing notions of identity via my profile pictures. I remember making my dad take me to see *The Rocky Horror Show* when I was 14. He wore a suit, as he wouldn't get dressed up with me, and I wore my mum's lingerie. We must've been a sight together!

I get my clothes from ebay mainly. I like to have full matching one-colour looks. And I tend to wear my favourite looks to death.

My first ever latex see-through Barbie dress (which I'm wearing in my 'going-out' photo) means the most to me of all the items of clothing I own. This dress was the starting point of me and my business partner Bo coming together and starting our latex fashion brand journey. There is nothing sexier than putting on a latex dress made to fit your body. It's so empowering.

Alis Pelleschi

I love being naked
and this is an evolution
of that. I love the idea
of becoming a real-life
version of archetypal
characters, such as
Barbie, internet porn
3D babes or a princess —
one of my hopes for
the future is to take
a trip to Disneyland to
live as a princess."

Alis Pelleschi

Marine Pierrot Detry *Music press officer & booking agent*

"Elegance in all its forms – it is not enough just to be well dressed –
is a marvellous spring of positive energy. Imagination rules the world."

"I'm not a snob about brands or labels – if I like a piece and it fits well then I grab it. I buy from a mixture of independent stores in Los Angeles and London, vintage stores, as well as some high-street stores for everyday pieces. Oh, and nothing excites me more than finding out a theatrical costumier is having a sale. Occasionally I will splash out on a designer piece – especially shoes. My favourites are a pair of custom-fitted silver snakeskin wedges by Terry de Havilland. He is a dear friend of mine and he named the shoe 'Esmé' after me.

I was always very spirited as a child, and definitely had my own ideas about how things should be done. My father is a real eccentric so I think I definitely got a healthy dose of that from him.

When I was around 15 I got into rock and metal music and became fascinated with the goth and fetish scenes. This was really a turning point for me in terms of starting to express myself through my personal style – I was so excited with how much I could say without even opening my mouth.

I do believe that identity defines what you choose to wear, and this idea is something that I love to explore through my work as an actress. You can say so much about a character through their wardrobe choices – but more importantly, your style can really affect the way you feel and behave.

The way I dress comes from the creativity of being an artist. I see my appearance as an expression of how I am feeling, which is why it can vary so much depending on my mood and which 'character' or facet of my personality is most prominent on any given day."

Esmé Bianco *Actress & burlesque performer*

David Motta *Fashion stylist*

"In colour psychology, pink is a sign of hope. It is a positive colour,
inspiring warm and comforting feelings, a sense that everything will be okay.
I like to think (I'm) pink!"

"I was born in London, but I have always regarded myself as Irish because as soon as I was seaworthy my parents had me on a boat back to Ireland. My parents – in particular my father – were strong republicans. My father was also a bodybuilding champion, a boxing champion, captain of the Irish football team and captain of the hurling team. Everyone knew him by name and me, his first-born and son, awkward, religious and far from interested in politics. From this non-conforming without realising it, came non-conforming with a purpose.

Before puberty my sole pleasures lay in God and my almost daily visits to the library in the village where I was brought up. I was on first-name terms with all the librarians, but had struck up an odd friendship with the oldest member of staff, Mary McGrath, who worked there part-time Monday, Wednesday and Thursday.

By the age of 11, I had read almost 80 per cent of the books in the children's section, so before my twelfth birthday Mary let me use the adult section of the library. This was the most exciting thing to happen to me in my young life. The adult section was a marvel: wood flooring smelling of polish, long tables with overhead lighting, and chairs for adults on which I could sit and swing my legs as I leafed through books with words I didn't understand and authors with names I couldn't pronounce.

I didn't know it at the time, but the books I read then, would help make me the person I am today. I go back and reread some of these books regularly. My favourites include Simone De Beauvoir's *She Came to Stay*, *The Well of Loneliness* by Radclyffe Hall and Jean Genet's *Our Lady of the Flowers*. These books not only changed the way I think and viewed my life and those around me, they gave me the strength to do this, telling me how to be comfortable in my awkward pre-teenage life and within 18 months I not only quoted passages from these books to my friends, family and teachers, I was also dressing as my amazing anti-heroes who lived in me through these amazing books."

Cornelius Brady *Artist & model*

Lou Bones *Membership manager*

Empress Stah *Circus & cabaret performer, producer & director*

"I'm a creative person; I enjoy aesthetics. If I dress the same as the masses, it makes me feel very uncomfortable like I'm not being true to myself.

In all the pictures of me as a child, I'm either dressed up as a fortune-teller or full tomboy, and always up to something, with a cheeky grin on my face.

I believe in wearing your personality on the outside. My style even changes with my mood. My mum says she can tell what's going on in my head by how I dress that day."

"I was born in small-town Australia. I have always demanded to dress myself and had my own style. As soon as I left my conservative high school I shaved my head and pierced my face – this was back in 1992. I also had a crew cut hair-do with a rat's tail when I was nine years old… it *was* the Eighties, though."

Arian Bloodwood *Community development accountant*

"I was born in Canberra, the capital of Australia. A totally planned city, the epitome of the 20th-century project of middle class suburbia. Aged seven, I got into trouble in school for taking my sewing project home and leaping ahead with it on my own. Year 11, I went to the school formal dressed as half-man half-woman: left side all beard, shirt, long trousers; right side clean face, make-up, blouse, skirt, stocking. Made the outfit myself. No one wanted to dance with me – too much for 1975 Canberra.

As soon as I left school I went to visit a friend in Sri Lanka, where the men all wear the *lungi* (sewn-up sarong). It was a revelation to be in a culture where trousers was a minority choice for men. I never looked back.

I still have the predecessor of my classic blouse, a top I made in 1979. It's of almost indestructible rayon (viscose), the colours still as fresh as new. I used to wear it all the time – sawmilling, welding, dancing under the stars, making love. It vividly evokes that part of my life.

I now have a little network of dressmakers and tailors who make up the designs I come up with. There's a symbiotic relationship between my identity and my clothes. Mostly a new garment or outfit or look comes to me as spontaneous inspiration, and I think, 'OMG, how can I wear that?!' Other times I see someone – usually a woman – wearing something on the street, and I think, 'How can I wear that, make it mine?'

So to wear that new outfit I have to reshape my identity to incorporate that. Sometimes it's back the other way: I will feel some internal energy or entity that I have not expressed, and then I mentally cast around for how I can express that.

Overall, the urge is to be me and to be seen to be me. To participate in social life as fully me and no one else.

Arian Bloodwood

I believe men can (and should) claim an expanded range of legitimated choices for ourselves and for all men – in the area of clothing and fashion, certainly, but also in the areas of emotional expressiveness, affectionate relationships, receptive pleasures and spiritual connection.

At one level wearing 'gender-non-conforming' clothes means that I have to be prepared to carry a large amount of energy on the street and in public: people look at me, have reactions to me (both intensely positive and intensely negative). As a result I enlarge my energy field somewhat, and so when people interact with me I usually engage from within that enlarged space, as though I am playing a slightly larger-than-life semi-impersonal role with them.

When people see me, I'd like them to think: 'There's a stylish and elegant man … What a great outfit … Oh, look – he's wearing a dress…' I'd love it if they notice how that disrupts and expands their conception of gender as a simple binary."

Arian Bloodwood

Lyall Hakaraia *Queerdom facilitator*

"If dressing up as Dracula for a whole month and starting my own cult in the playground at the age of eight is not conforming then we live in a very limited society."

About the author

Born in Coventry, England, Anthony Lycett studied photography at the Solihull College of Art & Technology and Coleg Sir Gar, Wales where he gained a BTEC HND (Distinction) in Photography.

Anthony's images have since been featured worldwide in publications such as *i-D*, *Vice*, *The Sunday Times Magazine*, *Saatchi Gallery Magazine*, *Flux*, *Vestal Magazine* (USA), *Wylde*, *The WILD*, *Citizen K* (France), *Lotto* (Germany), *Vision* (China) and *Eloquence* (South Korea). His advertising and corporate clients include M&C Saatchi, Karmarama, Republic clothing, TBWA and NatWest.

Among numerous accolades for Anthony's work, his *Forget Me Not* project, which focuses on his mother's ongoing experience of Alzheimer's disease, earned him the Portrait Series prize at the 2014 AOP Awards.

The first *Self.Styled* exhibition was held at Galerie Isabelle Gounod, Paris, January– February 2016.

Thanks

My mum and dad

Jo Sax

Amechi Ihenacho

Isabelle Caparros

Keith Parry

Deborah at Darkroom Digital

Isabelle Gounod

Magdalene Celeste

Byron Pritchard

Morana Tkalec

Arno Devo

Professor Christopher Breward

Everyone who has taken part in *Self.Styled*

Epigrams:

"I am me and not them." Louie Banks

"More is more." Glyn Fussell

"Something fresh, raw & filling, but no set menu."
 Gaffy Gaffiero

"Live solely & utterly in each rewarding moment
 of every day." Molly Parkin

"Always different & always a lot." Echo Morgan

"Desire to explore the deeper waters." Erika Dark

"Don't wear beige... it might kill you." Sue Kreitzman

"Charm & karma." Lyall Hakaraia

Images on pages 2 and 254:
Anne-Sophie Cochevelou